Knitting
a Kiss
in Every
Stitch

NICKY EPSTEIN

Knitting a Kiss in Every Stitch

Creating gifts
for the people you love

Nicky
Epstein
Books

An imprint of Sixth&Spring Books

To my husband, Howard, who often wisely tells
me to use the "KISS" rule: Keep It Simple, Sweetheart.

Managing Editor: Wendy Williams

Senior Editor: Michelle Bredeson

Art Director: Diane Lamphron

Yarn Editor: Tanis Gray

Technical Editor: Carla Scott

Instructions Editor: Eve Ng

Instructions Proofreaders:
Jordana Jacobs, Nancy Henderson,
Lori Steinberg, Lisa Buccellato

Technical Illustrations:
Jane Fay, Eve Ng

Copy Editor: Kristina Sigler

Vice President, Publisher:
Trisha Malcolm

Creative Director: Joe Vior

Production Manager:
David Joinnides

President: Art Joinnides

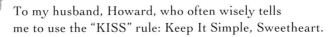

Cover and principle photography: Rose Callahan

Fashion Stylist: Laura Maffeo

Hair and Makeup: Elena Lyakir

Still-life Photography: Jack Deutsch Studio

Library of Congress Control Number: 2009931101
ISBN: 978-1-933027-86-9
Manufactured in China
1 3 5 7 9 10 8 6 4 2
First Edition

Contents

'Tis a gift to be simple,
'Tis a gift to be free,
'Tis a gift to come down
Where we ought to be...

–Shaker Hymn

Giving Gifts

It's nice to receive a gift, but it can be even more gratifying to give one. And as a knitter, I can't think of a more wonderful gift to give to loved ones, friends or those in need than a gift that you've knit yourself, with a kiss in every stitch.

When my stepson Scott was bravely recovering from a series of chemotherapy treatments, I knitted a cashmere cap for him to keep his handsome but bald head warm. He loved the cap, and I loved knitting it for him even more.

A handmade gift is so much more personal than a purchased gift because of the thought, time and affection that you've put into it. In this book there are gifts for babies, toddlers, boys and girls, teens, men, women, pets and friends, as well as gifts for charitable giving. For those of you generous knitters belonging to the thousands of groups worldwide who knit projects for charity, there's a list of organizations on page 118 and instructions on how to contact them. You'll learn what knitted gifts they accept and any special requirements for donating your projects.

When I was recently recovering from back surgery, I received a number of hand-knit gifts from friends and well-wishers and was genuinely touched by their thoughtfulness, because I knew how much work went into their creations.

As I was designing and knitting these projects I kept thinking of the beautiful Shaker hymn "Simple Gifts." I hope that these gifts will carry your message to that special person in your life, or make a person in need feel special.

Give of yourself…make someone happy… it's all about caring!

Nicky Epstein

chapter one
the kids

Baby's First Hat

MATERIALS
- 1 1.75oz/50g skein (each approx 136yds/124m) of *Mission Falls 136 Merino Superwash*, 100% merino wool superwash, each in #19 mist (A), #536 aster (B), #535 crocus (C), #531 sprout (D)
- Size 5 (3.75mm) needles, OR SIZE TO OBTAIN GAUGE
- Size 5 (3.75mm) double-pointed needles for cord top
- Tapestry needle

~~~~~~~~~~~

This hat has four edgings to choose from. But choose quickly...they grow up fast! See the Newborns in Need charity listed on page 120 for information on giving a cap to babes in need.

◼◼◼◻◻
EASY

Sizes
Preemie (Newborn, 6–9 months)

Finished measurements
Circumference 11 (13, 15)"/28 (33, 38)cm
Height 4¼ (5½, 7)"/11 (14, 18)cm

Gauge
24 sts and 24 rows = 4"/10cm in Garter st
TAKE TIME TO CHECK GAUGE

1. Rib with Daisies Hat
With A, cast on 68 (80, 92) sts.
Row 1 (RS) *P2, k4; rep from *, end p2.
Row 2 *K2, p4; rep from *, end k2.
Rep rows 1 and 2 for 1¼"/3.5cm.
Work in Garter st for 2½ (3¾, 5¼)"/6.5 (9.5, 13.5)cm.

CROWN SHAPING
Row 1 (RS) K1, *k2tog; rep from * to last st, k1— 35 (41, 47) sts.
Rows 2, 4 and 6 Knit.
Row 3 K1, *k2tog; rep from * to end—18 (21, 24) sts.
Row 5 Rep row 1 (3, 1)—10 (11, 13) sts.
Row 7 K0 (1, 1), *k2tog; rep from * to end—5 (6, 7) sts.
For 2nd and 3rd sizes only Purl, dec 1 (2) sts evenly across row—5 sts.

I-CORD TOP
Change to dpns and work I-cord (see page 123) for 1"/2.5cm.
Pass 2nd, 3rd, 4th and 5th sts over first st. Fasten off.
Work a 5-petal lazy daisy st (see page 125) over every other K4 rib section. Embroider a French knot (see page 125) in center of each flower.

2. Mini Curly Q Hat
With B, cast on 56 (66, 76) sts loosely.
Row 1 K into the front, back and front of each st to end—168 (198, 228) sts.

Bind off purlwise.
Following direction of spiral, tighten corkscrew to form 22 (26, 30) twists. With spare needle, pick up 1 st on each twist—22 (26, 30) sts.
With new needle, cast on 1 st, *k1 picked up st, cast on 2 sts; rep from *, end cast on 1 st—68 (80, 92) sts.
Work in Garter st for 3½ (4¾, 6¼)"/9 (12, 16)cm.

CROWN SHAPING AND I-CORD TOP
Work crown shaping and I-cord top same as Rib with Daisies Hat.

3. Double T-Twist Hat
**With C, cast on 68 (80, 92) sts. K 6 rows.
Next row (RS) *K6, rotate LH needle counter-clockwise 360 degrees; rep from * to last 2 sts, k2. Leave sts on needle.
With a 2nd needle, rep from **. Cont in garter st for 1¼"/3cm.
Hold both needles parallel with shorter piece in front, and using a 3rd needle, *k 1 st from front needle together with 1 st from back needle; rep from * to end—68 (80, 92) sts.
Work in Garter st for 2½ (3¾, 5¼)"/6.5 (9.5, 13.5)cm.

CROWN SHAPING AND I-CORD TOP
Work crown shaping and I-cord top same as Rib with Daisies Hat.

4. Bobble Hat
MB (Make Bobble) K in front, back, front, back, front of next st, turn, p5, turn, k5, turn, p5, turn, pass 2nd, 3rd, 4th and 5th sts over first st.
With D, cast on 68 (80, 92) sts.
Row 1 (WS) Knit.
Row 2 K3, *MB, k5; rep from * to last 5 sts, MB, k4.
Work in Garter st for 3½ (4¾, 6½)"/9 (12, 15)cm.

CROWN SHAPING AND I-CORD TOP
Work crown shaping and I-cord top same as Rib with Daisies Hat.

Finishing (all hats)
Sew back seam. Weave in ends. ❊

Woven Baby Blanket

MATERIALS
- 11 1.75oz/50g balls (each approx 95yds/87m) of *Trendsetter Yarns Scoubidu*, 50% cotton/50% acrylic, in #674 yellow stone wash (A)
- 12 balls in #660 purple stone wash (B)
- Size 8 (5mm) needles, OR SIZE TO OBTAIN GAUGE
- Size G (4mm) crochet hook
- Tapestry needle (optional)
- Washable clear permanent adhesive

◼◼◻◻
EASY

Finished measurements
Approx 24" x 36"/61 x 91.5cm

Gauge
16 sts and 14 rows = 4"/10cm in seed stitch
TAKE TIME TO CHECK GAUGE

Pattern stitches
SEED ST (ODD NUMBER OF STS)
Row 1 *K1, p1, rep from *, end k1.
Rep row 1 for pattern.

REVERSE SINGLE CROCHET
With RS facing, single crochet in each st working from left to right.

Horizontal strips for blanket
(make 12 with color B)
Cast on 11 sts. Work in seed st for 24"/61cm. Bind off.

Vertical strips for blanket
(make 9 with color A)
Cast on 11 sts. Work in seed st for 36"/91.5cm. Bind off.

Assembly
Place vertical strips on a flat surface. Weave horizontal strips over and under vertical strips. After all strips are woven, lightly glue centers of overlapping strips into place and let dry (or tack in place with yarn and tapestry needle).

Edging
With B and RS facing, start at one corner of blanket, *work 3 single crochet in corner, single crochet evenly across to next corner; rep from * 3 times more, join with sl st to first single crochet. Do not turn.
Work 1 row reverse single crochet evenly around, join with sl st to first sc. Fasten off. ✳

This lovely blanket is easily made using seed-stitch
strips woven together like the potholders we made as children.
Washable fabric glue helps hold the strips in place.

Go Girl Beaded Socks

Your special little girl will have the fanciest feet in the neighborhood, and will feel like a little princess (which she is).

INTERMEDIATE

One size
Child's Medium

Finished measurements
Approx 6"/15cm foot circumference
Approx 6½"/16.5cm from heel to toe

Gauge
32 sts and 46 rows = 4"/10cm in St st
TAKE TIME TO CHECK GAUGE

Special instruction
AB (add bead) With one bead on crochet hook, pick up st from left hand-needle and pull through bead; return st to left hand-needle and k st.

Leg
With smaller needles, cast on 48 sts. Divide sts evenly over 3 needles, pm and join, being careful not to twist stitches.
Rnd 1 *K2, p2; rep from * to end.
Rnd 2 *K1, AB, p2; rep from * to end.
Rnd 3 Rep Rnd 1.
Rnd 4 *AB, k1, p2; rep from * to end.
Rep Rnds 1–4 until leg measures 4"/10cm from beg.
Change to larger needles and k 1 rnd.

Heel flap
Sl last 12 sts on needle 3 to empty needle; with this needle, k12 from needle 1. Place rem 24 sts on hold for instep. Heel is worked over 24 sts. Turn.
Row 1 (WS) Sl 1, p to end.
Row 2 *Sl 1, k1; rep from * to end.
Rep Rows 1 and 2 until 24 rows are complete, end with Row 2.

Turn heel
Row 1 (WS) Sl 1, p11, p2tog, p1. Turn.
Row 2 Sl 1, k1, ssk, k1. Turn.
Row 3 Sl 1, p to 1 st before gap, p2tog, p1. Turn.
Row 4 Sl 1, k to 1 st before gap, k2tog, k1. Turn.
Rep Rows 3 and 4 until 14 sts remain.

Next row Rep row 3 once more.
Next row Sl 1, k to 1 st before gap, k2tog—12 sts.

Gussets
Cont with needle 1, pick up and k12 sts along side of heel; with needle 2, knit across 24 instep sts; with needle 3, pick up and k12 sts along other side of heel, k6 from needle 1—60 sts.
Rnd 1 K to last 3 sts on needle 1, k2tog, k1; k 24 sts on needle 2; k1, ssk, k to end of rnd.
Rnd 2 Knit.
Rep Rnds 1 and 2 until 48 sts rem.

Foot
Work even in St st until foot measures 5"/12.5cm or 1½"/4cm less than desired finished length.

Toe
Rnd 1 K to last 3 sts on needle 1, k2tog, k1; k1, ssk, k to last 3 sts on needle 2, k2tog, k1; k1, ssk, k to end of rnd.
Rnd 2 Knit.
Rep Rnds 1 and 2 until 16 sts rem.
With needle 3, k4 from needle 1.
Graft toe sts (see Kitchener stitch on page 124). ✳

Li'l Knitting Angel Hat

INTERMEDIATE

MATERIALS
- 1 1.75oz/50g ball (each approx 109yds/100m) of *RYC/Westminster Fibers, Inc. Silk Wool DK*, 50% merino wool/50% silk, each in #300 milk (A), #304 cord (B), #308 brownstone (C), #303 scallop (D)
- 1 .88oz/25g ball (each approx 82yds/75m) of *Rowan/Westminster Fibers, Inc. Kidsilk Aura*, 75% kid mohair/ 25% silk, each in #764 walnut (E), #752 wheat (F)
- Size 5 (3.75mm) needles, OR SIZE NEEDED FOR GAUGE
- Stitch markers
- Stitch holders
- Tapestry needle
- Small amounts of desired colors for eyes, nose, mouth and knitting
- Small amount of fiberfill
- Angel wings (approx 5½" x 6"/14 x 15cm) (available at most craft stores)
- ½ yd/m ½"/1.5cm white ribbon
- 48 round 5mm glass beads (24 per halo)
- 10"/25cm jewelry wire (5"/12.5cm each halo)
- Miniature knitting needles (2½"/6.5cm long) (available from Unicorn Books, Inc.)

Finished measurements
Approx circumference 15¼"/38.5cm
Approx height 9"/23cm

NOTE Miniature knitting needles can be made by gluing bead to top of pointed toothpick.

Gauge
20 sts and 28 rows = 4"/10cm in St st
TAKE TIME TO CHECK GAUGE

SPECIAL ABBREVIATION
LT (left twist) Skip first st on LH needle and k in back of 2nd st; k skipped st, dropping both sts off needle.

Pattern stitch
Mock cable rib (multiple of 4 sts plus 2)
Row 1 (RS) P2; *k2, p2; rep from * to end.
Row 2 K2, *p2, k2: rep from * to end.
Row 3 P2, *LT, p2; rep from * to end.
Row 4 Rep Row 2.
Rep Rows 1–4 for pattern.

Body
With A (C), cast on 78 sts. Work in mock cable rib for 12 rows, dec 1 st in last row—77 sts.
Set-up row (RS) K19, pm, k39, pm, k19. Work 3 rows in St st.
Dec row (RS) [K to 2 sts before marker, ssk, k2tog] twice, k to end.
Cont in St st, rep dec row every 4th row twice more—65 sts. Work 3 rows in St st. Remove markers.
Next row (RS) K15, ssk, k31, k2tog, k15—63 sts. P 1 row.

Front sleeves
Row 1 (RS) K16 and place these sts on one holder; k31 and place rem 16 sts on second holder; cast on 11 sts—42 sts.
Row 2 P42, cast on 11 sts—53 sts.
Row 3 K11, k2tog, k to last 13 sts, ssk, k11—51 sts.
Row 4 Purl.
Rep last 2 rows 6 times more—39 sts.
Bind off 14 sts at beg of next 2 rows. Place rem 11 sts on holder.

These whimsical hats double as hand puppets.

Your knitting angel can also trade her
needles for a magic wand
and become a fairy.

Back left sleeve

With RS facing, place 16 sts from first holder onto a spare needle ready for RS row. Attach second ball of A, k16, pm, pick up and k11 across cast on edge of front sleeve—27 sts.
Row 1 (WS) Purl.
Row 2 K to 2 sts before marker, ssk, k to end—26 sts.
Rep Rows 1 and 2 until 19 sts rem.
Next row K5 and place these sts on holder. Bind off rem 14 sts.

Back right sleeve

With RS facing, place 16 sts from 2nd holder onto a spare needle. With A, pick up and k11 across cast-on edge of sleeve, pm, k16—27 sts.
Row 1 Purl.
Row 2 K to marker, k2tog, k to end—26 sts.
Rep Rows 1 and 2 until 19 sts rem.

Next row Bind off 14 sts, k to end.
Place rem 5 sts on holder. Sew shoulder seams.

Head

With RS facing, place 21 sts from holders onto needle ready for RS row and attach B (D).
Row 1 (RS) Knit.
Row 2 Purl.
Row 3 *K1, m1, k1; rep from * to last st, k1—31 sts.
Work even in St st until head measures 1½"/4cm, end with a WS row.
Next row *K2tog; rep from * to last st, k1—16 sts.
Next row Purl.
Next row *K2tog; rep from * to end—8 sts. Cut yarn, leaving a long tail for sewing. Thread tail through rem sts, pull tight and secure.

Finishing
Face

Embroider face, using straight st for nose, eyebrows and mouth, French knots for eyes, referring to photo for placement.
Stuff head lightly with fiberfill and sew back of head seam. Sew seam at back of body. Tie ribbon around neck. Center wings at upper back and sew in place.

Hand (make 2)

With B (D), cast on 8 sts. Work in St st for 6 rows.
Next row (RS) *K2tog; rep from * to end—4 sts.
Cut yarn, leaving a long tail for sewing. Thread tail through rem sts, pull tight and secure. Sew seam and sew hand to end of sleeve. Sew sleeve opening closed.

Curls (make 9 long and 3 short for each angel)

With E (F), cast on 15 (10) sts.
Row 1 *K in front and back of st; rep from * to end—30 (20) sts.
Bind off purlwise. Twist to form curl. Sew short curls at front and long curls around back of head, tacking each curl at top and bottom.

Halo

String 24 pearls onto 5"/12.5cm of jewelry wire and twist ends tog. Attach to top of head.

Knitting

Using miniature needles, cast on 8 sts of desired color and work in garter st for 1"/2.5cm. Slip a needle through sts of each hand, keeping 4 sts on each needle. Roll a small ball of yarn and pin to ribbing. ✳

Reversible Hoodie

MATERIALS
• 1 3.5oz/100g skein (each approx 306yds/280m) of *Lion Brand LB Collection Superwash Merino*, 100% superwash merino, each in #98 antique (A) and #107 sky (B)
• Size 5 (3.75mm) needles, OR SIZE TO OBTAIN GAUGE
• Size 4 (3.5mm) double-pointed needles
• Tapestry needle

INTERMEDIATE

Sizes
6 mos (1 yr)

Finished measurements
Chest 21¼ (23)"/54 (58.5)cm
Length 9½ (10)"/24 (25.5)cm

Gauge
18 sts and 32 rows = 4"/10cm in pattern stitch
TAKE TIME TO CHECK GAUGE

Pattern stitch
Row 1 Knit.
Row 2 K1, *yo, k1; rep from * to end.
Row 3 K1, *drop yo from left-hand needle, k1; rep from * to end.
Rep Rows 2 and 3 for pattern.

NOTE Make one piece in each color.

Back
Cast on 48 (52) sts. Work in pattern for 5 (5½)"/12.5 (14)cm—20 (22) ridges.

Sleeves
Cast on 18 (20) sts at end of next 2 rows—84 (92) sts.
Cont in pattern for 3½"/9cm—14 ridges.

Neck
Work 33 (36) sts in pattern and slip these sts onto a holder for first front, bind off center 18 (20) sts for back neck. Cont in pattern on 33 (36) front sts for 1"/2.5cm—4 ridges.

Front
Cast on 11 (12) front neck sts—44 (48) sts. Work even until front sleeve measures same as back sleeve. Loosely bind off 18 (20) sts sleeve sts, then cont to work even on 26 (28) front sts until front measures same as back. Bind off. Join yarn to first front and work the same, reversing all shaping.

Hood
With RS facing, pick up and k17 (18) sts along first front and side neck, 28 (30) sts across back neck, and 17 (18) sts along other side and front neck—62 (66) sts. Work even in pattern for 7 (7½)"/18 (19)cm, ending with a Row 3—27 (29) ridges. K31 (33), then graft or sew top seam of hood loosely. Sew sleeve and side seams. With RS tog, join the two pieces with whip st along front and hood edges. Turn RS out, and join sleeve and bottom edges with whip st. Steam gently to align seams.

I-CORD (make 2)
With A and dpns, cast on 4 sts. Work in I-cord (see page 123) for 9"/23cm. Sew to each side of front neck. Knot ends of I-cords. ✤

This made-with-love sweater is sure to become an heirloom passed on for generations with remembrance of the knitter…you!

Be inventive and use a striped or variegated yarn for one side and a solid for the other.

Travelin' Man Hats

MATERIALS

3.5oz/100g skeins (each approx 170yds/156m) of *Lion Brand Yarn Vanna's Choice*, 100% acrylic, 1 skein each as follows:

1. Hit the Road Hat
- #300 denim mist (A)
- #305 pearl mist (B)
- Small amt of black yarn
- 3 micro mini plastic cars

2. Come Fly With Me Hat
- #304 seaspray mist (A)
- #305 pearl mist (B)
- 3 micro-mini plastic planes

For Both Hats:
- Size 9 (5.5mm) needles, OR SIZE NEEDED FOR GAUGE
- Tapestry needle

INTERMEDIATE

Finished measurements
Circumference 16"/40.5cm

Gauge
18 sts and 24 rows = 4"/10cm in St st
TAKE TIME TO CHECK GAUGE

1. Hit the Road Hat
With B, cast on 66 sts. Work in k2, p2 rib for 1¼"/3cm.
With A, work in St st for 5"/12.5cm.

CROWN SHAPING
Row 1 (RS) K1, *k2tog, k2; rep from * to last st, k1—50 sts.
Rows 2, 4 and 6 Purl.
Row 3 K1, *k1, k2tog; rep from * to last st, k1—34 sts.
Row 5 K1, *k2tog; rep from * to last st, k1—18 sts
Row 7 *K2tog; rep from * to end—9 sts.
Row 8 P1, *p2tog; rep from * to end—5 sts.
Row 9 Pass 2nd, 3rd, 4th and 5th sts over first st. Fasten off.
Sew back seam.

Hit the road or take to the sky. Youngsters will love these hats. One features mini toy cars sewn onto a knitted road, and the other has toy airplanes on a knitted sky.

Your little one is in
the driver's seat with this
"Hit the Road" hat!

ROAD
With B, cast on 5 sts. Work in St st for
15"/38cm. Bind off.

Finishing
Pin road around hat as desired and sew in
place. With black, weave in and out of every
2–3 rows along center of road. Attach cars
by sewing wheel axles onto the road.

With B, make a 2½"/6.5cm pompom (see
page 125) and attach to top of hat. ✳

The sky's the limit
for your best little
guy in this adorable
little topper; it comes
complete with
airplanes and clouds!

2. Come Fly With Me Hat
With B, cast on 66 sts. K 6 rows. With A,
work in St st for 5"/12.5cm.

CROWN SHAPING
Work same as Hit the Road Hat.

CLOUD
With B, work cloud chart in duplicate st at
center front of hat. Attach planes by sewing
wheel axles onto hat.

Make pompom same as for Hit the
Road Hat. ✳

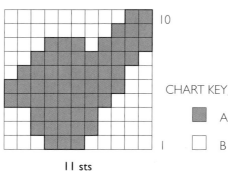

10

CHART KEY

▨	A
☐	B

1

11 sts

Curly Q Hat

MATERIALS

- 3.5oz/100g skeins (each approx 170yds/156m) of *Lion Brand Yarn Vanna's Choice*, 100% acrylic, 1 skein each in #301 rose mist (A), #124 toffee (B) and #158 mustard (C) (small amount used in the bobble)
- Size 9 (5.5mm) needles, OR SIZE NEEDED FOR GAUGE
- Tapestry needle
- 1 yd/92cm ribbon, ¾"/1cm wide

If your little girl is having a bad hair day, try this hat, complete with knitted curls and a flower embellishment.

EASY

Finished measurements
Circumference 16"/40.5cm

Gauge
18 sts and 24 rows = 4"/10cm in St st
TAKE TIME TO CHECK GAUGE

With A, cast on 66 sts. Work in St st for 6"/15cm, end with a WS row.

Hat
CROWN SHAPING
Row 1 (RS) K1, *k2tog, k2; rep from * to last st, k1—50 sts.
Rows 2, 4 and 6 Purl.
Row 3 K1, *k1, k2tog; rep from * to last st, k1—34 sts.
Row 5 K1, *k2tog; rep from * to last st, k1—18 sts.
Row 7 *K2tog; rep from * to end—9 sts.
Row 8 P1, *p2tog; rep from * to end—5 sts.
Row 9 Pass 2nd, 3rd, 4th and 5th sts over first st. Fasten off.
Sew back seam, reversing seam on bottom 1¼"/3cm for rolled edge.

Curls (make 8)
With B, cast on 16 sts very loosely.
Row 1 K in front, back and front of each st to end—48 sts.
Bind off purlwise.
Attach 4 curls to each side of hat. Cut ribbon in half and tie around each group of curls.

Flower
With A, cast on 38 sts.
Rows 1–4 Knit.
Row 5 (RS) *K6, rotate LH needle counter-clockwise 360 degrees; rep from * to last 2 sts, k2.
Row 6 *K2tog; rep from * to end—19 sts.
Row 7 K1, *k2tog; rep from * to end—10 sts.
Row 8 *K2tog; rep from * to end—5 sts.
Cut yarn and thread tail through rem sts, pull tightly and secure. Overlap last twist over first twist and sew in place.

Bobble
With C, cast on 1 st.
Row 1 (RS) K in front, back, front, back, front of st—5 sts.
Rows 2 and 4 Purl.
Row 3 Knit.
Row 5 K2tog, k1, k2tog—3 sts.
Row 6 P3tog.
Fasten off. Using tails, sew to center of flower. Sew flower to top of hat. ✻

POCKET Doodles For Kids

POCKETDoodles Kids

A playful guide for doodling, imagining, and coloring outside the lines.

BILL ZIMMERMAN

DRAWINGS BY TOM BLOOM

Heidi Hat

MATERIALS
• 3.5oz/100g skeins
(each approx 170yds/156m)
of *Lion Brand Yarn Vanna's
Choice*, 100% acrylic,
1 skein each in #303 purple
mist (A) and #158
mustard (B)
• Size 9 (5.5mm) needles,
OR SIZE NEEDED FOR
GAUGE
• Size 6 (4mm) double-
pointed needles (dpns)
• Tapestry needle
• 1 yd/92cm ribbon,
¼"/6mm wide

Finished measurements
Circumference 16"/40.5cm

Gauge
18 sts and 24 rows = 4"/10cm in St st
TAKE TIME TO CHECK GAUGE

With A, cast on 66 sts. Work in St st for
6"/15cm, end with a WS row.

Hat
CROWN SHAPING
Row 1 (RS) K1, *k2tog, k2; rep from * to last st,
k1—50 sts.
Rows 2, 4 and 6 Purl.
Row 3 K1, *k1, k2tog; rep from * to last st,
k1—34 sts.
Row 5 K1, *k2tog; rep from * to last st, k1—18 sts
Row 7 *K2tog; rep from * to end—9 sts.
Row 8 P1, *p2tog; rep from * to end—5 sts.
Row 9 Pass 2nd, 3rd, 4th, and 5th sts over first st.
Fasten off.
Sew back seam, reversing seam on bottom
1¼"/3cm for rolled edge.

Flower
With A, cast on 38 sts.
Rows 1–4 Knit.
Row 5 (RS) *K6, rotate LH needle counter-
clockwise 360 degrees; rep from * to last 2 sts, k2.
Row 6 *K2tog; rep from * to end—19 sts.
Row 7 K1, *k2tog; rep from * to end—10 sts.
Row 8 *K2tog; rep from * to end—5 sts.

Cut yarn and thread tail through rem sts, pull
tightly and secure. Overlap last twist over first
twist and sew in place.

Bobble
With C, cast on 1 st.
Row 1 (RS) K in front, back, front, back,
front of st—5 sts.
Rows 2 and 4 Purl.
Row 3 Knit.
Row 5 K2tog, k1, k2tog—3 sts.
Row 6 P3tog.
Fasten off. Using tails, sew to center of flower.
Sew flower to front of hat.

Pigtail braids (make 2)
With B and dpns, cast on 5 sts. Work I-cord
(see page 123) for 15"/38cm. Make 3 cords for
each braid. Braid 3 strands and tie ends with
ribbon, leaving 2"/5cm unbraided. Attach a braid
to each side of hat. ※

—ᨐᨐᨐ—

Charming braids adorn this pretty little cap, and
the easy rolled edges are a sweet finish!

Meow Kitty Cap

MATERIALS
- 1 1.75oz/50g ball (each approx 137yds/125m) of *Filatura di Crosa/Tahki•Stacy Charles, Inc. Zara Chiné*, 100% superwash merino wool, each in #1769 copper chiné (A) and #1764 cocoa chiné (B)
- Small amounts of black and white yarn for face embroidery
- 2 Size 6 (4mm) circular needles, each 16"/40cm long
- Size 4 (3.5mm) needles
- Size 6 (4mm) needles, OR SIZE NEEDED FOR GAUGE
- Size 6 (4mm) double-pointed needles (dpns)
- Stitch holders
- Size G-6 (4mm) crochet hook
- Small amount of fiberfill

The details on this clever cap make it extra-special for your kitty lover. It's the cat's meow!

INTERMEDIATE

One size
4–6 yrs

Finished measurements
Depth 9"/23cm
Height 10"/25.5cm

Gauge
22 sts and 32 rows = 4"/10cm over St st using larger needles
TAKE TIME TO CHECK GAUGE

Center back piece
With A and larger needles, cast on 12 sts.
Row 1 (WS) P5, pm, p2, pm, p5.
Row 2 (inc) K to first marker, m1, k2, m1, k to end—14 sts.
Row 3 Purl.
Rep rows 2 and 3 twenty times more—54 sts.
Next row K20. Turn, leaving rem 34 sts unworked.

Right ear
Work 3 rows in St st over these 20 sts.
Cont in St st, bind off 2 sts at beg of next 8 rows—4 sts.
Cont in St st, cast on 2 sts at beg of next 8 rows—20 sts.
Work in St st for 4 rows. Place sts on holder.

Left ear
With RS facing, skip center 14 sts and place rem 20 sts on needle. Join A and work same as right ear.

Front piece
With RS facing, circular needle and A, pick up and k31 sts along right-hand edge of center back piece to base of ear.
*Sl 5 sts from holder to dpn, sl next 5 sts to 2nd dpn and fold ear so 2nd dpn is behind first one.

[K one st on first dpn tog with one st on 2nd dpn] 5 times. Sl next 5 sts to dpn, sl foll 5 sts to 2nd dpn and fold ear so first dpn is behind 2nd one. Rep between [ ] 5 times.** Working between ears, k6, m1, k2, m1, k6; rep from * to ** for 2nd ear over next 20 sts. Pick up and k31 sts along left-hand edge—98 sts.

NOTE You will need to work back and forth with 2 circular needles at this point and can change to one circular needle, if desired, when there are enough rows to comfortably do so.

Row 1 (WS) With B, p37; with A, p24; with B, p37.
Row 2 With B, k37; with A, k11, m1, remove marker, k2, remove marker, m1, k11; with B, k37—100 sts.
Rows 3–6 With A, work in St st.
Row 7 With B, p36; with A, p28; with B, p36.
Row 8 With B, k38; with A, k24; with B, k38.
Row 9 With B, p39; with A, p22; with B, p39.
Row 10 With B, k40; with A, k20; with B, k40.
Rows 11–14 With A, work in St st.
Row 15 With B, p34; with A, p32; with B, p34.
Row 16 With B, k37; with A, k26; with B, k37.
Row 17 With B, p38; with A, p24; with B, p38.
Row 18 With B, k39; with A, k22; with B, k39.
Rows 19–22 With A, work in St st.
Row 23 With B, p35; with A, p30; with B, p35.
Row 24 With B, k39; with A, k22; with B, k39.
Row 25 With B, p40; with A, p20; with B, p40.
Row 26 With B, k41; with A, k18; with B, k41.
Rows 27–30 With A, work in St st.
Row 31 With B, p45; with A, p10; with B, p45.
Row 32 With B, k46; with A, k8; with B, k46. Cut B.
Row 33 With A, *p2, p2tog; rep from * to end—75 sts.
Change to smaller needles and work in k1, p1 rib for 1"/2.5cm. Bind off sts in rib.

Meow Kitty Cap
back view

Finishing
Using duplicate st, stem st and chain st, embroider face on front of hat using photo as guide.

Back band
With RS facing, smaller needles and B, pick up and k77 sts evenly across back edge of hat. Work in k1, p1 rib for 1"/2.5cm. Bind off in rib.

Ties (make 2)
With dpns and B, cast on 7 sts for ball, leaving a long tail for seaming.
Row 1 (RS) *K in front and back of next st; rep from * to end—14 sts.
Rows 2, 4, 6, 8 and 10 Purl.
Rows 3, 5, 7 and 9 Knit.
Row 11 [K3tog] 4 times, k2tog—5 sts.

Work in I-cord (see page 123) for 8½"/21.5cm, or desired length. Bind off.

Stuff ball with fiberfill. Thread cast-on tail through cast-on sts and gather; sew side seam. Sew bound-off edge of one tie to each end of back band.

With crochet hook and A, work a row of sc around each ear, joining front and back edges. ❊

Creatures of the Nightcaps

MATERIALS

1.75oz/50g balls (each approx 136yds/123m) of *Lane Borgosesia/Trendsetter Yarns Merino 6-ply*, 100% wool, 1 as follows:

1. Vampire Bite Cap
• 2 balls #20266 grey (A)
Small amounts of
• #11 black (B)
• #60 red (C) and
• #1 white (D)

2. Werewolf Cap
1 ball each
• #20964 charcoal (A) and
• #60 red (B)

• Size 6 (4mm) needles,
OR SIZE NEEDED
TO OBTAIN GAUGE
• Size 5 (3.75mm) needles
• Tapestry needle

INTERMEDIATE

One size

Small/Medium (increase needle size by one to knit large version)
Dircumference Approx 19"/48cm
Depth Approx 8"/20.5cm

Gauge

20 sts and 28 rows = 4"/10cm in St st using larger needles
TAKE TIME TO CHECK GAUGE

NOTE Instructions are given for chart pats to be worked in intarsia. Chart pats can also be worked in duplicate stitch if desired.

1. Vampire Bite Cap

With A and smaller needles, cast on 100 sts. Work in St st for 1½"/24cm, end with a RS row. K 1 WS row for turning ridge. Change to larger needles. K 1 RS row. Continue in St st for 22 rows more.
Next row K39, work 22 sts of chart, k39.
Cont in St st, working rem 17 rows of chart. Then work 7 more rows in A.

Werewolves and vampires are all the rage with the tween and teen set. These "bite me" caps will warm the most cold-blooded of creatures.

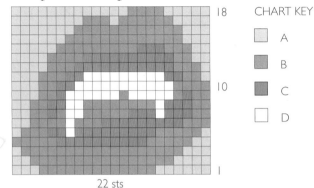

For the "Plain Janes," simply knit the
hat and leave off the vampire bite.

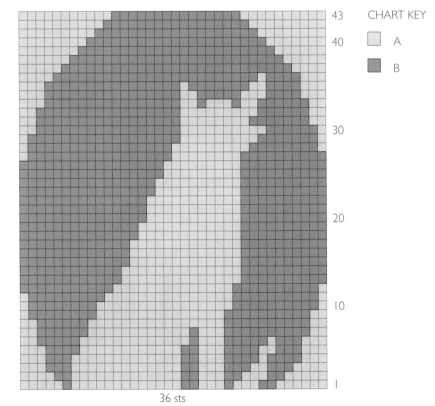

CROWN SHAPING

Row 1 (RS) *K2tog, k8;
rep from * to end—90 sts.
Row 2 and all WS rows Purl.
Row 3 *K2tog, k7; rep from * to end—80 sts.
Row 5 *K2tog, k6; rep from * to end—70 sts.
Row 7 *K2tog, k5; rep from * to end—60 sts.
Row 9 *K2tog, k4; rep from * to end—50 sts.
Row 11 *K2tog, k3; rep from * to end—40 sts.
Row 13 *K2tog, k2; rep from * to end—30 sts.
Row 15 *K2tog, k1; rep from * to end—20 sts.
Row 17 *K2tog; rep from * to end—10 sts.
Break yarn and thread tail through rem sts.
Pull tight to gather and secure.

Embroider blood drops using lazy daisy st (see
page 125). Sew back seam. Fold hem to inside
of hat at turning ridge and sew in place.

2. Werewolf Cap

With A and smaller needles, cast on 100 sts.
Work in St st for 1"/2.5cm, end with a RS row.
K 1 WS row for turning ridge. Change to
larger needles. K 1 RS row. Cont in St st
for 3 rows.
Next row K32, work chart over next
36 sts, k32.
Cont in St st working rem 42 rows of chart.
Work 1 purl row in A.

CROWN SHAPING

Work same as Vampire Bite Cap.
Break yarn and thread tail through rem sts.
Pull tight to gather and secure.

Sew back seam. Fold hem to inside of hat at
turning ridge and sew in place.�✺

Vampire Bite Cap

CHART KEY

A
B
C
D

22 sts

Werewolf Cap

CHART KEY

A
B

36 sts

Slouchy Bow Hat

MATERIALS
- 2 1.75oz/50g balls (each approx 195yds/178m) of *Crystal Palace Yarns Mini-Mochi*, 80% superwash merino wool/20% nylon, in #108 neptune rainbow
- Size 7 (4.5mm) 16"/40cm circular needle, OR SIZE NEEDED TO OBTAIN GAUGE
- Size 7 (4.5mm) double-pointed needles (dpns)
- Size 5 (3.75mm) 16"/40cm circular needle
- Stitch marker
- Tapestry needle

This gift comes with its own bow! It's the perfect hat for your favorite teenager or your hippest girlfriend.

EASY

Sizes
Small/Medium (Large/XL)

Finished Measurements
Circumference Approx 21 (24)"/53.5 (61)cm
Depth Approx 9½ (10½)"/24 (26.5)cm

Gauge
20 sts and 28 rows = 4"/10cm in pat st
TAKE TIME TO CHECK GAUGE

Hat
With smaller needle and 2 strands held together, cast on 72 (80) sts. Pm and join, being careful not to twist stitches.
Work in k2, p2 rib for 1"/2.5cm.
Inc rnd *K2, yo, p2, yo; rep from * to end—108 (120) sts.

Change to larger circular needle.
Rnds 1 and 2 *K2, p2; rep from * to end.
Rnds 3 and 4 *K1, p2, k1; rep from * to end.
Rnds 5 and 6 *P2, k2; rep from * to end.
Rnd 7 and 8 *P1, k2, p1; rep from * to end.
Rep Rnds 1 and 2 once more. Then work pat in reverse, from Rnd 8 to 1, until hat measures 8½ (9½)"/21.5 (26.5)cm from beg, end with a Rnd 7.

CROWN SHAPING
NOTE Change to dpns when necessary.
Rnd 1 *[P2, k2] twice, p2, k2tog; rep from * to end—99 (110) sts.
Rnd 2 *P2, k2, p2, k2tog, p2, k1; rep from * to end—90 (100) sts.
Rnd 3 *P2, k2tog, [p2, k1] twice; rep from * to end—81 (90) sts.
Rnd 4 *[P2, k1] twice, p2tog, k1; rep from * to end—72 (80) sts
Rnd 5 *P2, k1, p2tog, k1, p1, k1; rep from * to end—63 (70) sts.

Rnd 6 *P2tog, k1, [p1, k1] twice; rep from * to end—54 (60) sts.
Rnd 7 *K2tog; rep from * to end—27 (30) sts.
Rnd 8 K1 (0), *k2tog; rep from * to end—14 (15) sts.
Rnd 9 K0 (1), *k2tog; rep from * to end—7 (8) sts.
Break yarn. Thread tail through rem sts, pull tight to close opening and secure.

Bow
With one strand and smaller needle, cast on 14 sts. Work in St st for 6½"/16.5cm. Bind off. Sew ends together to form a ring.

Tie
With one strand and smaller needle, cast on 3 sts. Work I-cord (see page 123) for 2"/5cm. Bind off. Flatten bow with seam at bottom center and wrap tie tightly around center. Sew ends of tie together at bottom. Attach bow to ribbing of hat. ※

chapter two
the girls

All Heart Shawl

MATERIALS

- 1 3.5oz/100g hank (approx 127yds/116m) of *Classic Elite Yarns Montera*, 50% llama/50% wool, in #3819 rose quartz (MAKE 8)

- 1 1.75oz/50g hank (approx 120yds/110m) of *Classic Elite Yarns Portland Tweed*, 50% virgin wool/25% alpaca/25% viscose, in #5054 barely there lilac (MAKE 7)

- 1 1.75oz/50g hank (approx 108yds/99m) of *Classic Elite Yarns Premiere*, 50% pima cotton/50% tencel, in #5271 jasmine (MAKE 6)

- 2 1.75oz/50g balls (approx 75yds/69m) of *Classic Elite Yarns Duchess*, 40% merino wool/28% viscose/10% cashmere/7% angora/15% nylon, in #1071 keepsake pink (MAKE 10)

- 1 1.75oz/50g hank (approx 100yds/91m) of *Classic Elite Yarns Solstice*, 70% organic cotton/30% merino wool, in #2319 petal (MAKE 5)

- 1 1.75oz/50g ball (approx 110yds/101m) of *Classic Elite Yarns Pebbles*, 75% cotton/25% acrylic, in #2871 bermuda sand (MAKE 4)

- 1 1.5oz/42g ball (approx 90yds/82m) of *Classic Elite Yarns La Gran*, 76½% mohair/17½% wool/6% nylon, in #6519 cameo pink (MAKE 3)

- 1 1.5oz/42g ball (each approx 90yds/82m) of *Classic Elite Yarns La Gran*, 76½% mohair/17½% wool/6% nylon, each in #63536 frosty orchid and #61532 positively pink (MAKE 6 EACH)

- 2 1.5oz/42g balls (each approx 90yds/82m) of *Classic Elite Yarns La Gran*, 76½% mohair/17½% wool/6% nylon, in #6571 Julia's pink (A) (MAKE 6)

- NOTE Use needle sizes indicated on yarn ball bands.

- Washable clear permanent adhesive

- Size G-6 (4mm) crochet hook

- Tapestry needle

INTERMEDIATE

Finished measurements
Approx 16" x 64"/40.5 x 160cm (61 hearts)

Gauge
Varies by yarn. See yarn ball bands.

Hearts
Make various size and gauge hearts in either stockinette or seed stitch in the number indicated after each yarn listed.

STOCKINETTE ST HEARTS
Cast on 3 sts. With a separate ball of yarn, cast on 3 more sts onto same needle—6 sts.
Row 1 (RS) *[K1, m1] twice, k1; rep on second set of sts—5 sts each set.
Row 2 and all WS rows Purl.
Row 3 *K1, m1, k to last st, m1, k1; rep on second set of sts—7 sts each set.
Row 5 and 7 Rep row 3—11 sts each set after Row 7.
Row 9 (joining row) *K1, m1, k9, k2tog, k9, m1, k1—23 sts. Cut second yarn.
Row 11 Knit.
Row 13 and all RS rows through Row 29 K1, ssk, k to last 3 sts, k2tog, k1—5 sts after Row 29.
Row 31 K1, sk2p, k1—3 sts.
Row 33 Sk2p—1 st.
Fasten off.

Ya gotta have hearts. Lots and lots and lots of hearts. This is a fun project for a group of knitters to create as a gift for a special person who has touched their hearts.

You can make the shawl any width
or length your heart desires. Just add
or subtract hearts.

SEED ST HEARTS
Seed St
Row 1 *P1, k1; rep from *, end p1.
Row 2 P the k sts and k the p sts.
Rep Row 2 for pattern.

NOTES Use backward loop cast-on at
beg, middle or end of rows. Work increased
sts into pat.

Cast on 3 sts. With a separate ball of yarn,
cast on 3 more sts onto same needle—6 sts.
Row 1 (RS) *[K1, m1] twice, k1; rep on
second set of sts—5 sts each set.
Row 2 and all WS rows Seed st.
Row 3 *Cast on 1 st, work in seed st to end,
cast on 1 st; rep on second set of sts—7 sts
each set.
Row 5 and 7 Rep Row 3—11 sts each set
after Row 7.
Row 9 (joining row) *Cast on 1 st, work 10
sts in seed st, k2tog, work 10 sts in seed st,
cast on 1 st—23 sts. Cut second yarn.

Row 11 Work in seed st.
Row 13 and all RS rows through Row 29
Ssk, work in seed st to last 2 sts, k2tog—5 sts
after Row 29.
Row 31 K1, sk2p, k1—3 sts.
Row 33 Sk2p—1 st.
Fasten off.

Finishing
Weave in ends and block lightly.
Assemble hearts into 2 panels, each approx
16 x 32"/40.5 x 81.5cm.

Starting at top of panel (center), place 3 large
hearts overlapping at sides. Randomly place
remaining hearts, overlapping to fit within
panel. Tack together using matching yarns or
fabric adhesive. Join panels along top edges of
large hearts by sewing the top 3 hearts of
each panel together.

With crochet hook and A, sc evenly around
entire shawl, working 3 sc at each heart point
at ends of shawl. Join with sl st in first sc.
Fasten off. ❊

• make it special
You can sew two
hearts together and
stuff with fiberfill or
potpourri to create a
unique valentine.

Bride's Purse

MATERIALS
• 1 1.75oz/50g ball (approx 109yds/100m) of *RYC/ Westminster Fibers, Inc. Silk Wool DK*, 50% silk/50% merino wool, in #300 milk (A)
• 1 1.75oz/50g ball (approx 137yds/125m) of *RYC/ Westminster Fibers, Inc. Pure Silk DK*, 100% silk, in #151 bone (B)
• 1 .88oz/25g ball (approx 229yds/210m) of *Rowan/ Westminster Fibers, Inc. Kidsilk Haze*, 70% super kid mohair/30% silk, in #634 cream (C)
• Size 5 (3.75mm) needles, OR SIZE TO OBTAIN GAUGE
• Size 4 (3.5mm) double-pointed needles (dpns)
• 2 cable needles
• Crystallized Swarovski Elements Crystal Pearls, style #001, color #650 white pearl: (10) 7mm, (26) 8mm, (5) 10mm, (5) 12mm, (5) 14mm
• Jewelry wire for handle
• ½ yd/.5m satin fabric for lining
• Small amount of fiberfill
• Tapestry needle

INTERMEDIATE

Finished measurements
Approx 9¼" × 9¼"/23.5 × 23.5cm

Gauge
36 sts and 35 rows = 4"/10cm in cable patterns on larger needles
TAKE TIME TO CHECK GAUGE

Pattern stitches
OPEN CABLE (OVER 10 STS)
3-st RPC Sl 2 to cn and hold to *back*, k1, p2 from cn.
3-st LPC Sl 1 to cn and hold to *front*, p2, k1 from cn.
4-st RPC Sl 1 to cn and hold to *back*, sl 2 to 2nd cn and hold to back, k1, move first cn to front, p2 from 2nd cn, k1 from first cn.
Row 1 (WS) K3, p1, k2, p1, k3.
Row 2 P3, sl 1 wyib, k2, sl 1 wyib, p3.
Row 3 K3, sl 1 wyif, k 2, sl 1 wyif, k3.
Row 4 P1, 3-st RPC, p2, 3-st LPC, p1.
Rows 5 and 7 K1, p1, k6, p1, k1.
Row 6 P1, k1, p6, k1, p1.
Row 8 P1, sl 1 wyib, p6, sl 1 wyib, p1.
Row 9 K1, sl 1 wyif, k6, sl 1 wyif, k1.
Row 10 P1, 3-st LPC, p2, 3-st RPC, p1.
Rows 11, 12 and 13 Rep Rows 1, 2 and 3.
Row 14 P3, 4-st RPC, p3.
Rep rows 1–14 for pattern.

COIN CABLE (OVER 9 STS)
5-st RC Sl 1 st to cn and hold to *back*, sl 3 sts to 2nd cn and hold to *back*, k1, move first cn to front, k3 from 2nd cn, k1 from first cn.
Rows 1 and 3 (WS) K2, p5, k2.
Row 2 P2, k5, p2.
Row 4 P2, sl 1 wyib, k3, sl 1 wyib, p2.
Row 5 K2, sl 1 wyif, p3, sl 1 wyif, k2.
Row 6 P2, 5-st RC, p2.
Rows 7 and 8 Rep Rows 1 and 2.
Rep Rows 1–8 for pattern.

Body
With A and larger needles, cast on 74 sts.
Row 1 K1, work coin cable, k1, *work open cable, k1, work coin cable, k1; rep from * to end.
Cont in patterns as established for 17"/43cm.

This bridal bag combines a contemporary look with an old tradition of accepting money from wedding guests to help pay for the honeymoon.

You can vary the amount of flowers, pearls and balls to suit the bride's taste.

Front flap

Work even in patterns as established for 2½"/6.5cm more, end with a WS row.
Dec row (RS) K1, ssk, work in patterns to last 3 sts, k2tog, k1.
Rep dec row every RS row until 48 sts rem. Bind off 2 sts at beg of next 8 rows. Bind off.

Flowers (make 3)

With 1 strand each of B and C held together and larger needles, cast on 101 sts.
Row 1 (WS) Purl.
Row 2 K2, *k1 and sl this st back to left-hand needle, with right-hand needle lift next 8 sts, one st at a time, over this st and off the needle, (yo) twice, k this st again, k2; rep from * to end.
Row 3 P1, *p2tog, drop first yo of previous row, k in front, back, front, back, front of rem yo, p1; rep from *, end p1.
Row 4 Knit.
Bind off knitwise.
To shape flower, roll bound-off edge to form a spiral and sew in place. Sew an 18mm pearl to the center of one flower, a 10mm pearl to center of the second flower and an 8mm to the third.

Cord balls (make 4)

With one strand each of B and C held together and larger needles, cast on 8 sts, leaving a long tail for sewing.
Row 1 (RS) K in front and back of every st—16 sts.
Row 2 and all WS rows Purl.
Rows 3, 5, 7, 9 and 11 Knit.
Row 13 *K2tog; rep from * to end—8 sts.
Row 14 *P2tog; rep from * to end—4 sts.
Change to dpns and work I-cord (see page 123) to 2½"/6.5cm, 4"/10cm, 6"/15cm and 7"/18cm or desired lengths. K4tog and fasten off.

Thread cast-on tail through cast-on sts, stuff balls with fiberfill and sew side seams. Sew one 8mm pearl to the end of each ball.

I-CORD FLAP EDGING

With one strand each of B and C held together and dpn, cast on 4 sts and work I-cord for 16"/40.5cm. Bind off.

PEARL HANDLE

Cut a 16"/40.5cm length of jewelry wire and string pearls as follows:
7 6mm, 5 7mm, 3 8mm, 2 10mm, 2 12mm, and 5 14mm; 2 12mm, 2 10mm, 3 8mm, 5 7mm, 7 6mm. Loop jewelry wire on each end and sew to bag.

Finishing

Cut lining and sew to fit inside bag. With WS together, sew to inside edges of bag. Measure 9"/23cm from cast-on edge for fold. Sew side seams. Sew I-cord around edge of bag flap. Weave 2 strands of A held together through the knit sts around bag opening, gather and knot, leaving a 7"/17.5cm opening. Sew 8mm beads to the center of open cables on bag front, flowers onto flap, and attach cord balls as pictured. ✻

OPEN CABLE

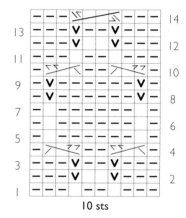

10 sts

COIN CABLE

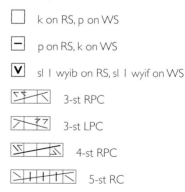

9 sts

CHART KEY

☐	k on RS, p on WS
─	p on RS, k on WS
V	sl 1 wyib on RS, sl 1 wyif on WS
	3-st RPC
	3-st LPC
	4-st RPC
	5-st RC

Cable Delight Hat

MATERIALS
- 2 3.5oz/100g hanks (each approx 45yds/41m) of *Blue Sky Alpacas Bulky*, 50% alpaca/50% wool, in
Hat A
- #1212 grasshopper (A)
Hat B
- #1213 jasmine (B)
Hat C
- #1215 claret (C)
Hat D
- #1000 angora (D)
- Size 15 (10mm) 16"/40cm circular needle, OR SIZE TO OBTAIN GAUGE
- Size 15 (10mm) double-pointed needles (dpns)
- Size 11 (8mm) double-pointed needles (dpns)
- Stitch marker
- Cable needle
- Tapestry needle
- Assorted brooches, beads or buttons (optional)

■■□□□
EASY

Sizes
Small (Medium)

Finished circumference
17 (18¾)"/43 (47.5)cm to fit up to 22 (24)"/56 (61)cm head

Gauge
8 sts and 10 rows = 4"/10cm in St st
TAKE TIME TO CHECK GAUGE

Pattern stitch
Cable panel (over 14 sts)
4-st RC Sl 2 sts to cn and hold to *back*, k2, k2 from cn.
4-st LC Sl 2 sts to cn and hold to *front*, k2, k2 from cn.
4-st RPC Sl 2 sts to cn and hold to *back*, k2, p2 from cn.
4-st LPC Sl 2 sts to cn and hold to *front*, p2, k2 from cn.

Cable panel
Rnds 1, 2, 4, 5 and 6 P1, k2, p2, k4, p2, k2, p1.
Rnd 3 P1, k2, p2, 4-st RC, p2, k2, p1.
Rnd 7 P1, 4-st LPC, 4 st RC, 4-st RPC, p1.
Rnds 8 and 18 P3, k8, p3.
Rnd 9 P3, 4-st RPC, 4-st LPC, p3.
Rnds 10 and 16 P3, k2, p4, k2, p3.
Rnd 11 P1, 4-st RPC, p4, 4-st LPC, p1.
Rnds 12, 13 and 14 P1, k2, p8, k2, p1.
Rnd 15 P1, 4-st LPC, p4, 4-st RPC, p1.
Rnd 17 P3, 4-st LC, 4-st RC, p3.
Rnd 19 P1, 4-st RPC, 4-st RC, 4-st LPC, p1.

Rnd 20 P1, k2, p2, k4, p2, k2, p1.

Basketweave (multiple of 4 sts)
Rnds 1 and 2 *K2, p2; rep from *.
Rnds 3 and 4 *P2, k2; rep from *.
Rep Rnds 1–4 for pattern.

Hat
With circular needles, cast on 40 (44) sts. Pm and join, being careful not to twist sts.
Rnds 1 and 2 P1 [k2, p2] 3 times, k0 (2), work cable panel (starting with Rnd 1), k0 (2) [p2, k2] 3 times, p1.
Rnds 3 and 4 K1, [p2, k2] 3 times, p0 (2), work cable panel, p0 (2), [k2, p2] 3 times, k1.
Cont to work in Basketweave and Cable panel as established until Rnd 20 of Cable panel has been completed.

CROWN SHAPING
Change to dpns when necessary.
Rnd 1 P1, [k2tog, p2] 3 times, k 0 (2) tog, work Rnd 1 of cable panel, k 0 (2)tog, [p2, k2tog] 3 times, p1—34 (36) sts.
Rnd 2 P1, [k1, p2] 3 times, k0 (1), work Rnd 2 of cable panel, k0 (1), [p2, k1] 3 times, p1.
Rnd 3 K1, [p1, k2tog] 3 times, p0 (1), work Rnd 3 of cable panel, p0 (1), [k2tog, p1] 3 times, k1—28 (30) sts.
Rnd 4 K1 [p1, k1] 3 times, p0 (1), work Rnd 4 of cable panel, p0(1), [k1, p1] 3 times, k1.
Rnd 5 Sl 0 (1) st to end of needle 3, [k2tog] 3 times, [p2tog, k2tog] twice, [k2tog, p2tog] twice, [k2tog] 3 (4) times—14 (15) sts.
Rnd 6 [K2tog] 7 (6) times, [k3tog] 0 (1) time—7 sts.

The hat can be enhanced with a favorite pin, vintage or new. Or just go for a classic cable look.

Angora (D)

Claret (C)

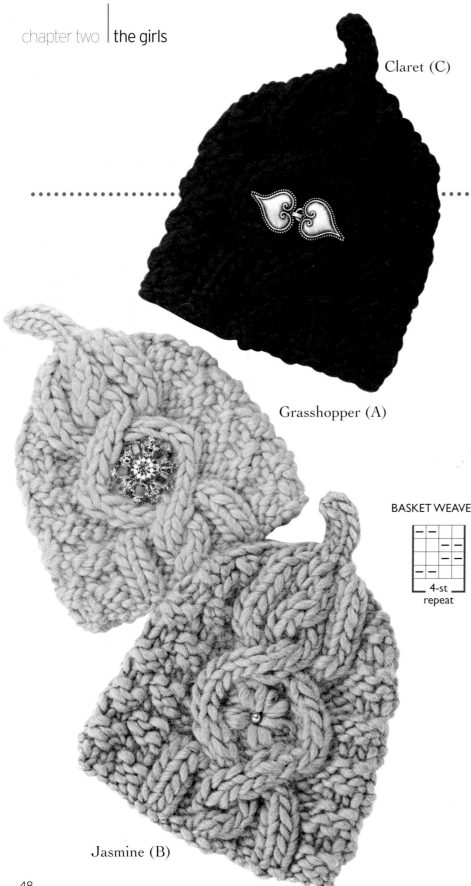

Grasshopper (A)

Jasmine (B)

I-CORD TOP
Change to smaller dpns.
Rnd 7 K2tog, k3, k2tog—5 sts.
Rnds 8–11 Work in I-cord (see page 123) for 4 rows.
Rnd 12 K2tog, k1, k2 tog—3 sts.
Rnd 13 Sk2p.
Fasten off.

• **Grasshopper A** Embellish center of open cable with your favorite pin.
• **Jasmine B** Embroider lazy daisy st to center of open cable and sew bead to center.
• **Claret C** Embellish center of open cable with button or clasp.
• **Angora D** Leave hat plain or embroider

CABLE PANEL

BASKET WEAVE ST

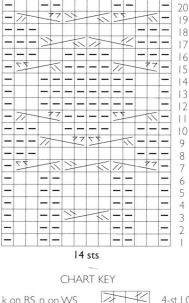

4-st repeat

14 sts

CHART KEY

☐ k on RS, p on WS		4-st LC
— p on RS, k on WS		4-st RPC
4-st RC		4-st LPC

Diamond Rib Wrap

MATERIALS
• 11 1.75oz/50g hanks (each approx 150yds/137m) of *Fairmount Fibers, Ltd./Manos del Uruguay Silk Blend Semi Solids*, 30% silk/70% merino wool, in #300S magenta

• Size 8 (5mm) needles, OR SIZE TO OBTAIN GAUGE

• Tapestry needle

• Pewter clasp (available at *nickyknits.com*)

Size
Each panel measures approx 18" × 44"/45.5 × 112cm

Gauge
20 sts and 28 rows = 4"/10cm in St st

Pattern stitches
Slip st rib (multiple of 5 sts + 2)
Row 1 (RS) P2, *k1, sl 1, k1, p2; rep from *.
Row 2 K2, *p3, k2; rep from *.
Rep Rows 1 and 2 for pattern.

Diamond panel (over 59 sts)
Row 1 (RS) [P2, k2] 3 times, p2, *[m1, p1] twice, p1, [k2, p2] 3 times; rep from * to end.
Row 2 [K2, p2] 3 times, k2, *[p1, k1] twice, k1, [p2, k2] 3 times; rep from * to end.
Row 3 [P2, k2] 3 times, p2, *m1, p1, k1, p1, m1, p2, [k2, p2] 3 times; rep from * to end.
Row 4 [K2, p2] 3 times, k2, *[p1, k1] twice, p1, k2, [p2, k2] 3 times; rep from * to end.
Row 5 [P2, k2] 3 times, p2, *m1, [p1, k1] twice, p1, m1, p2, [k2, p2] 3 times; rep from * to end.
Row 6 [K2, p2] 3 times, k2, *[p1, k1] 4 times, k1, [p2, k2] 3 times; rep from * to end.
Row 7 [P2, k2] 3 times, p2, *m1, [p1, k1] 3 times, p1, m1, p2, [k2, p2] 3 times; rep from * to end.
Row 8 [K2, p2] 3 times, k2, *[p1, k1] 5 times, k1, [p2, k2] 3 times; rep from * to end.
Row 9 [P2, k2] 3 times, p2, *m1, [p1, k1] 4 times, p1, m1, p2, [k2, p2] 3 times; rep from * to end.

Row 10 *K1, kfb, sl 10, pass first slipped st over other 9, k2, [p1, k1] 5 times, p1; rep from * to last 14 sts, k1, kfb, sl 10, pass first slipped st over other 9, k2.
Row 11 [P2, k2] 3 times, p2, *ssk, [p1, k1] 3 times, p1, k2tog, p2, [k2, p2] 3 times; rep from * to end.
Row 12 [K2, p2] 3 times, k2, *[p1, k1] 5 times, k1, [p2, k2] 3 times; rep from * to end.
Row 13 [P2, k2] 3 times, p2, *ssk, [p1, k1] twice, p1, k2tog, p2, [k2, p2] 3 times; rep from * to end.
Row 14 [K2, p2] 3 times, k2, *[p1, k1] 4 times, k1,

Show someone how much you care with this go-anywhere wrap. It's fun to make and speaks volumes about the affection that you feel for a friend or relative.

The cozy cuffs can be made longer if desired.

[p2, k2] 3 times; rep from * to end.
Row 15 [P2, k2] 3 times, p2, *ssk, p1, k1, p1, k2tog, p2, [k2, p2] 3 times; rep from * to end.
Row 16 [K2, p2] 3 times, k2, *[p1, k1] 3 times, k1, [p2, k2] 3 times; rep from * to end.
Row 17 [P2, k2] 3 times, p2, *ssk, p1, k2tog, p2, [k2, p2] 3 times; rep from * to end.
Row 18 [K2, p2] 3 times, k2, *[p1, k1] twice, k1, [p2, k2] 3 times; rep from * to end.
Row 19 [P2, k2] 3 times, p2, *s2kp, p2, [k2, p2] 3 times; rep from * to end.
Row 20 [K2, p2] 3 times, k2, *p1, k2, [p2, k2] 3 times; rep from * to end.
Rep Rows 1–20 for diamond pattern.

Left front/back
Cast on 113 sts. Work 27 sts in Sl st rib, pm, work 59 sts in Diamond pat, pm, work rem 27 sts in Sl st rib. Cont in pats as established until piece measures 44"/112cm from beg. Bind off.

Right front/back
Work same as Left front/back.

Place panels side by side, matching cast-on and bound-off edges, and mark center point of panels for shoulder line. Sew back seam from cast-on edge to marked point.

Sleeves
Mark center 12"/30.5cm of left piece. With RS facing, pick up and k72 sts within marked width. Work in Sl st rib for 5"/12.5cm. Bind off. Repeat for right piece.

Finishing
Sew side and sleeve seams.
Block lightly.
Sew clasp to front opening. ✳

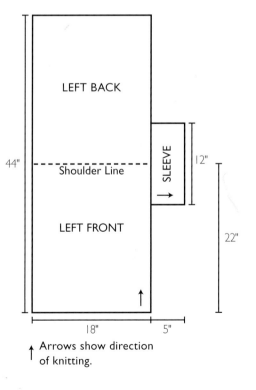

Arrows show direction of knitting.

Summer of Love Bag

MATERIALS
- 4 1.75oz/50g balls (each approx 120yds/111m) of *Berroco, Inc. Suede*, 100% nylon, in #3717 Wild Bill Hickcock (A)
- 1 ball in #3729 Zorro (B)
- Size 8 (5mm) needles, OR SIZE TO OBTAIN GAUGE
- Size 8 (5mm) double-pointed needles
- One pair 30"/76cm leather handles (Homestead Heirlooms sewn round leather core)
- Tapestry needle

Finished measurements
Approx 12" x 18"/30.5 x 46cm

Gauge
19 sts and 28 rows = 4"/10cm in Rev St st
TAKE TIME TO CHECK GAUGE

Body
With A, cast on 120 sts. Work in Rev St st for 18". Bind off.

Assembly
Cast-on and bound-off edges become the sides of the bag, and the side edges of the piece become the top of the bag. Fold the piece in half. With WS (knit side) tog, sew side seams to 3"/7.5cm from top edge.

Peace sign
With dpns and B, cast on 5 sts. Work in I-cord (see page 123) for 21"/53.5cm. Make 2 more cords 6"/15cm each. Using photo as guide, form peace sign and sew in place.

Finishing
Thread two strands of yarn held together through top front edge of bag, gather to 9½"/24cm width, and secure ends. Repeat for top back edge of bag. Mark side edge of bag 2"/5cm from bottom, bring

corners of bag to meet and sew in place.
Repeat on other side.
Sew handles to front and back.

Fringe
For each fringe, cut 5 strands of A 20"/51cm long. Fold in half, insert loop end through bottom edge of bag and draw ends through loop. Rep across bottom edge. Trim ends. ✳

This easy, uniquely crafted faux-suede
bag is a gift that's all about peace and love.

Legwarmer Trio

MATERIALS

1. Zip It

- 4 1.75oz/50g balls (each approx 103yds/94m) of *Berroco, Inc. Geode*, 50% wool/50% acrylic, in #3658 iron zebra
- Size 7 (4.5mm) needles, OR SIZE TO OBTAIN GAUGE
- 2 12"/30.5cm black separating zippers (art F-43 Coats & Clark sport zipper)
- Sewing needle and matching thread
- Tapestry needle
- Two leather tassels (optional)

MATERIALS

2. Button Up

- 2 3.5oz/100g hanks (each approx 183yds/167m) of *Tahki Yarns/Tahki•Stacy Charles, Inc. Donegal Tweed*, 100% pure new wool, in #862 denim
- Size 8 (5mm) needles, OR SIZE TO OBTAIN GAUGE
- Twelve 1"/2.5cm buttons (JHB#10185 Courtly)
- Tapestry needle

MATERIALS

3. Fur Up

- 2 3.5oz/100g hanks (each approx 215yds/198m) of *Berroco, Inc. Ultra Alpaca*, 50% super fine alpaca/50% Peruvian highland wool, in #6235 fuchsia (A)
- 6 .4oz/10g balls (each approx 70yds/64m) of *Berroco, Inc. Lazer FX*, 100% polyester, in #6008 black/black (B)
- 1 1.75oz/50g hank (approx 50yds/46m) of *Berroco, Inc Zap*, 100% polyester, in #3534 pitch black (C)
- Size 8 (5mm) needles, OR SIZE TO OBTAIN GAUGE
- Tapestry needle

EASY

Finished measurements

Length:
Zip-It 14"/35.5cm
Button Up 14"/35.5cm
Hot Stuff 12"/30.5cm
Circumference:
Zip It 12"/30.5cm
Button Up 12"/30.5cm
Hot Stuff 14"/35.5cm

1. Zip It
Gauge

28 sts and 26 rows = 4"/10cm in Rib pat
TAKE TIME TO CHECK GAUGE

Cast on 98 sts loosely.
Row 1 (WS) *K3, p2; rep from * to last 3 sts, k3.
Row 2 *P3, k2; rep from * to last 3 sts, p3.
Rep Rows 1 and 2 for Rib pat for 12"/30.5cm or desired circumference to fit around leg. Bind off.

Finishing

Sew zipper into cast-on and bound-off edges, easing edges to fit zipper. Attach leather tassel or yarn tassel to each zipper pull. ✳

- **here's a hint**
Baste or use fabric adhesive to hold zipper in place before stitching.

Same pattern, three different looks! Knit a pair for every gal on your gift list. These cozy warmers can be worn over jeans, boots or tights.

Zip It

Button Up

3. Fur Up
Gauge
24 sts and 24 rows = 4"/10cm in Rib pat with
A and B held together
TAKE TIME TO CHECK GAUGE

Starting at lower edge with one strand each
of A and B held together, cast on 83 sts.

Work Rib pat same as for Zip It Legwarmers
for 12"/30.5cm. Bind off loosely in pat.

With RS facing and 2 strands C held together,
pick up and k38 sts along side edge. K 4 rows.
Bind off. Sew side seams with C trim on
outside as pictured. ✳

2. Button Up
Gauge
28 sts and 26 rows = 4"/10cm in
Rib pat
TAKE TIME TO CHECK GAUGE

Work same as Zip It Legwarmers
for 13"/33cm. Bind off loosely in pat.
Overlap cast-on and bound-off
edges by 1"/2.5cm to form a tube
and sew in place. Sew 6 buttons
evenly spaced along seam. ✳

● **make it special**
These legwarmers can also be
worn as a hat and necklette.
How cool is that?

Fur Up

City Lights Beaded Scarf

MATERIALS
- 1 8oz/227g hank (each approx 750yds/686m) of *Interlacements New York*, 100% rayon, in #307 tapestry
- Size 5 (3.75mm) needles, OR SIZE TO OBTAIN GAUGE
- 1300 glass beads (size 6/0) in lt topaz
- sewing needle (materials kits available from *vintagestyles.com*)

INTERMEDIATE

Finished measurements
Approx 4" x 32"/10 x 81.5cm, excluding fringe

Gauge
28 sts and 42 rows = 4"/10cm in garter st
TAKE TIME TO CHECK GAUGE

Stitch pattern
SB Slide bead against last st and tighten.

Scarf
STRING BEADS
Using a sturdy thread, loop it through a folded piece of yarn and then pull both ends of thread through the eye of the needle. Pass the bead over the needle and thread it onto the yarn.

FRINGE CAST-ON
*Cast on 1 st, slide 20 beads to last st, keeping loop tight, cast on 1 st; rep from * 13 times more—28 sts and 14 loops.

Rows 1–20 *K4, sb; rep from * to last 4 sts, k4.
Rows 21 and 22 K5, sb, k3, sb, [k4, sb] 3 times, k3, sb, k5.
Rows 23 and 24 K6, sb, k2, sb, [k4, sb] 3 times, k2, sb, k6.
Rows 25 and 26 K7, sb, k1, sb, [k4, sb] 3 times, k1, sb, k7.
Rows 27–34 K8, sb, [k4, sb] 3 times, k8.
Rows 35 and 36 K9, sb, k3, sb, k4, sb, k3, sb, k9.
Rows 37 and 38 K10, sb, k2, sb, k4, sb, k2, sb, k10.
Rows 39 and 40 K11, sb, k1, sb, k4, sb, k1, sb, k11.
Rows 41 and 42 K12, sb, k4, sb, k12.
Rows 43 and 44 K13, sb, k2, sb, k13.
Row 45 K14, sb, k14.
Rep Row 45 for 24"/61cm.
Then work Rows 1–44 in reverse (start with Row 44 and end with Row 1).

FRINGE BIND-OFF
K1, *slide 20 beads to last st, keeping loop tight, [k1, pass first st over second st] twice (2 sts bound off); rep from *, end last rep bind off 1 st—14 loops.

Finishing
Weave tails into work, using sewing needle and matching thread to anchor ends. ✻

Beautiful silk ribbon yarn and beads come together easily to create this gift that keeps on giving every time it's worn.

Cable-and-Leaf Tote

MATERIALS
• 5 3.5oz/100g hanks
(each approx 100yds/91m)
of *Blue Sky Alpacas Worsted
Hand Dyes,* 50% alpaca/50%
merino in #2002 green
• Size 9 (5.5mm) needles,
OR SIZE TO OBTAIN
GAUGE
• Size 7 (4.5mm) needles
• Size H-8 (5mm) crochet
hook
• Cable needle
• Stitch holders
• Tapestry needle
• Small amount of smooth
waste yarn
• Wood handles (10⅞" x
7¼"/27.5 x 18.5cm; Sunbelt
Fastener Co., #W02
• Fabric for lining (optional)
• Sewing needle and
matching thread (optional)

▰▰▰▱
INTERMEDIATE

Finished measurements
Approx 16" x 12"/40.5 x 30.5cm, without handles
and casing

Gauge
16 sts and 22 rows = 4"/10cm in St st on larger
needles
TAKE TIME TO CHECK GAUGE

Pattern stitches
GK (Gordian Knot) Sl 4 sts to cn and hold to
front, k2, sl 2 purl sts back to left-hand needle,
bring cn with rem 2 knit sts to back, p2, k2 from cn.

Front
With larger needles, cast on 52 sts.
Set-up row (WS) P5, [(k2, p2) twice, k2, p6] twice,
[k2, p2] twice, k2, p5.
Row 1 (RS) K5, [(p2, k2) twice, p2, k6] twice, [p2,
k2] twice, p2, k5.
Row 2 Cast on 2 sts, k1, p6, [(k2, p2) twice, k2, p6]
twice, [k2, p2] twice, k2, p5.
Row 3 Cast on 2 sts, p1, k6, [p2, GK, p2, k6] 3
times, p1.
Row 4 Cast on 2 sts, p1, k2, [p6, (k2, p2) twice, k2]
3 times, p6, k1.
Row 5 Cast on 2 sts, k1, p2, [k6, (p2, k2) twice, p2]
3 times, k6, p2, k1.
Row 6 Cast on 2 sts, k1, p2, k2, [p6, (k2, p2) twice,
k2] 3 times, p6, k2, p1.
Row 7 Cast on 2 sts, p1, k2, p2, [k6, (p2, k2) twice,
p2] 3 times, k6, p2, k2, p1.

Row 8 Cast on 2 sts, p1, k2, p2, k2, [p6, (k2, p2)
twice, k2] 3 times, p6, k2, p2, k1.
Row 9 Cast on 2 sts, k1, p2, k2, p2, [k6, (p2, k2)
twice, p2] 3 times, k6, p2, k2, p2, k1.
Row 10 Cast on 2 sts, k1, [p2, k2] twice, [p6, (k2,
p2) twice, k2] 3 times, p6, k2, p2, k2, p1.
Row 11 Cast on 2 sts, p1, [k2, p2] twice, [k6, (p2,
k2) twice, p2] 3 times, k6, [p2, k2] twice, p1.
Row 12 Cast on 2 sts, p1, [(k2, p2) twice, k2, p6] 4
times, [k2, p2] twice, k1.
Row 13 Cast on 2 sts, k1, [p2, GK, p2, k6] 4 times,
p2, GK, p2, k1.
Row 14 Cast on 2 sts, p3, [(k2, p2) twice, k2, p6] 4
times, [k2, p2] twice, k2, p1.
Row 15 Cast on 2 sts, k3, [(p2, k2) twice, p2, k6] 4
times, [p2, k2] twice, p2, k3.
Row 16 Cast on 2 sts, p5, [(k2, p2) twice, k2, p6] 4
times, [k2, p2] twice, k2, p3.
Row 17 Cast on 2 sts, k5, [(p2, k2) twice, p2, k6] 4
times, [p2, k2] twice, p2, k5—84 sts.
Rows 18, 20 and 22 P5, [(k2, p2) twice, k2, p6] 4
times, [k2, p2] twice, k2, p5.
Rows 19 and 21 K5, [(p2, k2) twice, p2, k6] 4
times, [p2, k2] twice, p2, k5.
Rows 23, 33, 43 and 53 K5, [p2, GK, p2, k6] 4
times, p2, GK, p2, k5.
Rows 24–32, 34–42, 44–52 and 54–57 Rep Rows
18 and 19.
Row 58 Rep Row 18.
Row 59 K3, ssk, [(p2, k2) twice, p2, k4, ssk] twice,
[p2, k2] twice, p2, [k2tog, k4, (p2, k2) twice, p2]
twice, k2tog, k3—78 sts.
Row 60 P4, [(k2, p2) twice, k2, p5] 4 times, [k2,
p2] twice, k2, p4.

〰〰〰

A small detail can make a big difference in design. The leaf/cord
appliqué makes this carry-all (great for knitters) *très* chic.

Cable-and-Leaf Tote
back view

Row 61 K2, ssk, [(p2, k2) twice, p2, k3, ssk] twice, [p2, k2] twice, p2, [k2tog, k3, (p2, k2) twice, p2] twice, k2tog, k2—72 sts.
Row 62 P3, [(k2, p2) twice, k2, p4] twice, [k2, p2] twice, k2, [p4, (k2, p2) twice, k2] twice, p3.
Row 63 K1, ssk, [p2, GK, p2, k2, ssk] twice, p2, GK, p2, [k2tog, k2, p2, GK, p2] twice, k2tog, k1—66 sts.
Row 64 P2, [(k2, p2) twice, k2, p3] 4 times, [k2, p2] twice, k2, p2.
Row 65 Ssk, [(p2, k2) twice, p2, k1, ssk] twice, [p2, k2] twice, p2, [k2tog, k1, (p2, k2) twice, p2] twice, k2tog—60 sts.
Row 66 P1, *k2, p2; rep from * to last 3 sts, k2, p1.
Place sts on holder.

Back

Work same as front.

Gusset

With crochet hook and waste yarn, ch 4. With larger needles, pick up and k2 sts in center 2 back loops of chain. P 1 row.
Row 1 (WS) Purl.
Row 2 *K in front and back of st; rep from * to end—4 sts.
Rows 3, 5 and 7 Purl.
Rows 4, 6 and 8 K1, m1, k to last st, m1, k1—10 sts after row 8.
Work even in St st until piece fits around outside edge of front to start of decreases, end with a WS row.
Rows 1, 3 and 5 (RS) K1, ssk, k to last 3 sts, k2tog, k1—4 sts after Row 5.
Rows 2, 4 and 6 Purl.
Row 7 Ssk, k2tog—2 sts.
Row 8 Purl.
Place sts on holder.

Finishing

Sew gusset to front and back. Remove waste yarn from gusset cast-on and place one st on front holder and one st on back holder. Repeat for other end of gusset—62 sts each on front and back holders.

Handle casing

Place 62 sts from front holder onto smaller needles. With RS facing join yarn.
Row 1 (RS) K2, *p2, k2; rep from * to end.
Row 2 P2, *k2, p2; rep from * to end.
Rep Rows 1 and 2 for 20 rows total. Bind off. Insert casing through handle slot and sew bound-off edge to beg of rib. Repeat for back.

Leaf

With dpns, cast on 7 sts.
Row 1 (RS) K3, yo, k1, yo, k3—9 sts.
Row 2 and WS rows unless noted Purl.
Rows 3 and 9 K3, yo, k3, yo, k3—11 sts.
Rows 5 and 11 K3, yo, k5, yo, k3—13 sts.
Rows 7 and 13 Bind off 3 sts, k2, yo, k1, yo, k6—12 sts.

Rows 8 and 14 Bind off 3 sts, p8—9 sts.
Row 15 K3, yo, k3, yo, k3—11 sts.
Row 17 K3, yo, k5, yo, k3—13 sts.
Row 19 Bind off 4 sts, [k1, yo] twice, k6—11 sts.
Row 20 Bind off 4 sts, p6—7 sts.
Row 21 Ssk, yo, s2kp, yo, k2tog—5 sts.
Row 23 Ssk, k1, k2tog—3 sts.
Row 25 Sk2p—1 st.
Fasten off.

Corded leaf

With dpns, cast on 4 sts. Work in I-cord (see page 123) for 12½"/32cm.
Next row (RS) Cast on 1 st, [k1, cast on 1 st] 3 times—7 sts.
Next row Purl.
Work 25 rows of leaf.

Sew leaf and corded leaf to front of bag, using photo as guide. Line bag if desired. ✳

Lace Friendship Shawl

INTERMEDIATE

Finished measurements
Each panel measures approx
20" × 35"/51 × 89cm

Gauge
20 sts and 28 rows = 4"/10cm in lace pat after light blocking
TAKE TIME TO CHECK GAUGE

Left front/back
Using the long tail cast-on method, cast on 105 sts. K 2 rows.
Row 1 (RS) K2, ssk, *yo, k1, yo, k2, [k2tog] twice, k2; rep from * to last 2 sts, yo, k2.
Row 2 and all WS rows K2, p to last 2 sts, k2.
Row 3 K2, ssk, *yo, k3, yo, k1, [k2tog] twice, k1; rep from * to last 2 sts, yo, k2.
Row 5 K2, ssk, *yo, k5, yo, [k2tog] twice; rep from * to last 2 sts, yo, k2.
Row 7 K2, ssk, *yo, k3, k2tog, k2, yo, k2tog; rep from * to last 2 sts, yo, k2.
Row 8 Rep Row 2.
Rep Rows 1–8 for 35"/89cm ending with a Row 7. K 2 rows. Bind off kwise on WS.

Right front/back
Work same as Left front/back.

Place panels side by side, matching cast-on and bound-off edges, and mark center point of panels for shoulder line. Sew back seam from bound-off edge to marked point.

MATERIALS
• 6 1.75oz/50g hanks (each approx 219yds/200m) of *Knitpicks Imagination,* 50% superwash merino wool/25% superfine alpaca/25% nylon, in looking glass
• Size 7 (4.5mm) needles, OR SIZE TO OBTAIN GAUGE
• Tapestry needle
• Fleur-de-Lis Clasp (available at *nickyknits.com*)

This easy-wearing and flattering style is knit in two simple lace panels sewn together at the back. The sleeve cuffs pull it all together in high style.

Lightweight elegance for any occasion. Spice it up with a special closure.

Cuffs

Mark center 9"/23cm of each side.
With RS facing, pick up and k50 sts within marked width. Work in St st for 2"/5cm, end with a WS row.
Dec row K1, k2tog, k to last 3 sts, ssk, k1.
Rep dec row every 4th row 5 times more—38 sts.
Cont even in St st until cuff measures 7½"/19cm or desired length. Bind off loosely. Repeat on other side.
Sew cuff seams, reversing seam in last ¾"/2cm of cuff.

Block lightly to show lace pattern. ✽

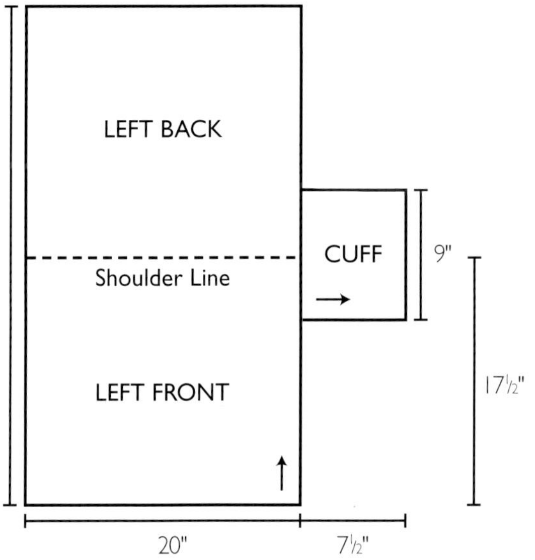

LEFT BACK

35"

Shoulder Line

CUFF

9"

LEFT FRONT

17½"

20"

7½"

↑ Arrows show direction of knitting.

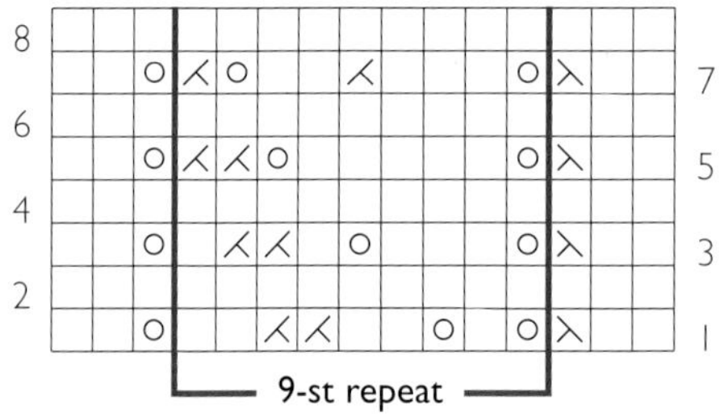

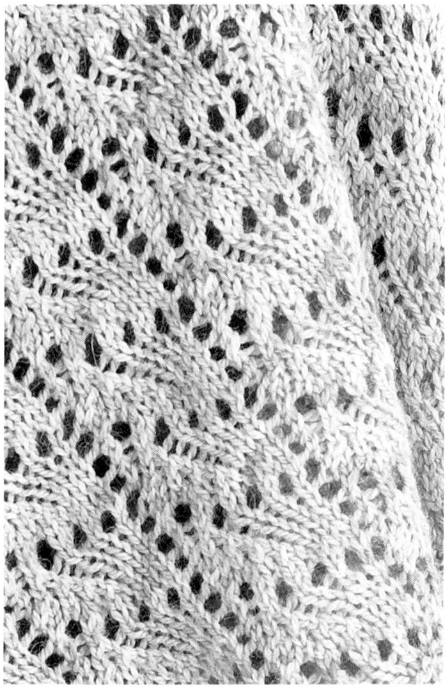

● make it special
The shawl can be made longer by adding length to the lace panels.

CHART KEY

☐ k on RS, p on WS

╱ k2tog

╲ ssk

○ yo

9-st repeat

Ruched Mitts

MATERIALS
- 1 1.75oz/50g ball (approx 120yds/110m) of *GGH/Muench Maxima*, 100% extra fine superwash merino wool, in #35 ruby (A)
- 1 .88oz/25g ball (approx 150yds/137m) of *GGH/Muench Soft-Kid*, 70% super kid mohair/5% wool/25% nylon, in #85 ruby (B)
- Size 6 (4mm) needles, OR SIZE TO OBTAIN GAUGE
- Size 3 (3.25mm) needles
- Size 8 (5mm) needles
- Tapestry needle
- 18 faceted glass beads (5mm)
- Sewing needle and matching thread

Sizes
Small (Medium)

Finished measurements
Length 11"/28cm
Wrist circumference 6¼ (8)"/16 (20.5)cm

Gauge
22 sts and 28 rows = 4"/10cm in St st on middle-sized needles

Cuff
With B and largest needles, cast on 68 (88) sts.
Work St st for 1¾"/4.5cm, end with a WS row.
**Change to smallest needles.
Dec row (RS) With A, *k2tog; rep from * to end—34 (44) sts.
K 5 rows.*** Change to largest needles.
Inc row (RS) With B, *kfb; rep from * to end—68 (88) sts.
Work in St st for 1½"/4cm, end with a WS row.
Rep from ** once more, then rep from ** to ***—34 (44) sts.

Change to middle-sized needles and work St st for 5"/13cm. Bind off.

Finishing
Sew side seam from cast-on edge to 1"/2.5cm into St st section. Leaving a 2"/5cm opening for thumb, sew remainder of seam, reversing seam on last 1"/2.5cm to allow edge to roll.

With B, embroider 3 flowers on each mitt as pictured (see page 125). Sew 3 beads at center of each flower. ❀

With their unique gathered cuffs and delicate embroidery, these mitts make a lovely and cozy gift.

Easy Opera Wrap

MATERIALS
• 4 (5) 3.5oz/100g balls (each approx 87yds/80m) of *Cascade Yarns Lana Grande*, 100% Peruvian wool, in #6034 red
• Size 19 (15mm) needles, OR SIZE TO OBTAIN GAUGE
• Stitch markers
• Tapestry needle
• Drama Clasp (available at *nickyknits.com*)

This quick knit gift is a theatrical show stopper, especially if you accessorize it with my new comedy-tragedy mask clasps.

INTERMEDIATE

Sizes
S/M (L/XL)

Finished measurements
Approx 37 (45)"/94 (114.5)cm square, before assembly

Gauge
6 sts and 12 rows = 4"/10cm in Garter st
TAKE TIME TO CHECK GAUGE

Body
Cast on 56 (68) sts very loosely.
Row 1 (RS) *P2, k2tog, yo, k2; rep from * to last 2 sts, p2.
Row 2 *K2, p2tog, yo, p2; rep from * to last 2 sts, k2.
Rep Rows 1 and 2 for 5 (6½)"/12.5 (16.5)cm.
Work in Garter st for 5½ (7½)"/14 (19)cm, mark ends of row for beg of armhole.
Cont in Garter st for 16 (17)"/40.5 (43)cm, mark ends of row for end of armhole.
Work in Garter st for 5½ (7½)"/14 (19)cm, end with a WS row.
Rep Rows 1 and 2 for 5 (6½)"/12.5 (16.5)cm.
Bind off very loosely in pattern.

ARMHOLE BANDS
With RS facing, pick up and k28 (30) sts evenly along 16 (17)" armhole edge between markers. Bind off loosely. Repeat on other side.

Fold piece in half so cast-on and bind-off rows meet with WS together. Sew side and armhole band seams. Sew clasp to front opening where desired. ✳

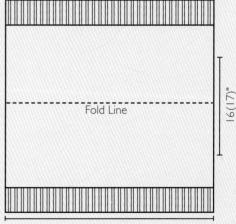

Fold Line

16 (17)"

37 (45)"

chapter three
the guys

Fisherman's Gloves

INTERMEDIATE

Sizes
Small (Medium/Large) Shown in M/L
Upper palm circumference 7 (8)"/18 (20.5)cm
Finished length 7 (8)"/18 (20.5)cm

Gauge
32 sts and 44 rows = 4"/10cm in St st
TAKE TIME TO CHECK GAUGE

Pattern stitches
K1, p1 double broken rib
(over an even number of sts)
Rnd 1 (RS)*K1, p1; rep from * to end.
Rnds 2–8 Rep Row 1.
Rnd 9 *P1, k1; rep from * to end.
Rnds 10-16 Rep Row 9.
Rep Rows 1–16 for pattern.

Seed st
Rnd 1*K1, p1; rep from * to end.
Rnd 2 P the k sts and k the p sts.
Rep Rnd 2 for pattern.

Cuff
Cast on 56 (64) sts loosely. Divide sts over
3 dpns, pm and join.
Work 24 rows in K1, p1 double broken rib.

Lower palm
Set up rnd K28 (32), pm, m1, pm, k28 (32).
Inc rnd K to marker; sl marker, m1, k to marker,
m1, sl marker, k to end.
Cont in St st, work inc rnd every 3rd rnd 7 (9)
times more—73 (85) sts; 17 (21) gusset sts
between markers.

Next rnd K to marker, remove marker, slip gusset
sts onto waste yarn, remove marker, cast on 1 st
to bridge gap, k to end—57 (65) sts.
Work even in St st until palm measures 3¼
(3¾)"/8.5 (9.5)cm above ribbing.

Little finger
K7 (8), place next 44 (50) sts onto waste yarn,
cast on 2 sts to bridge gap, k to end—15 (17) sts.
Arrange sts over 3 dpns and work in St st for ¾
(1)"/2 (2.5)cm. Work 3 rnds Seed st. Bind off
loosely in pat.

Upper palm
Place 44 (50) held sts onto 3 dpns. Pick up
and k1 at base of little finger, k44 (50), pick up and
k1 at base of little finger—46 (52) sts.
Work 2 (4) rnds in St st.

Ring finger
K8 (9), place next 30 (34) sts onto waste yarn,
cast on 2 sts to bridge gap, k8 (9)—18 (20) sts.
Arrange sts over 3 dpns and work in St st for 1
(1¼)"/2.5 (3)cm. Work 3 rnds Seed st.
Bind off loosely in pat.

Middle finger
Place 30 (34) held sts onto 3 dpns. Pick up and k1
at base of ring finger, k7 (8), place next 16 (18) sts
onto waste yarn, cast on 2 sts to bridge gap, k7
(8), pick up and k1 at base of ring finger—18 (20)
sts. Arrange sts over 3 dpns and work in St st for 1
(1¼)"/2.5 (3)cm. Work 3 rnds Seed st. Bind off
loosely in pat.

Index finger
Place rem 16 (18) sts onto 3 dpns. Pick up and k1
at base of middle finger, k16 (18), pick up and
k1 at base of middle finger—18 (20) sts. Arrange
sts evenly over 3 dpns and work in St st for 1
(1¼)"/2.5 (3)cm. Work 3 rnds Seed st.
Bind off loosely in pat.

Thumb
Place 17 (21) gusset sts onto 3 dpns. Pick up and
k1 at base of thumb, k17 (21)—18 (22) sts.
Work in St st for ¾ (1)"/2 (2.5)cm. Work 3 rnds
Seed st. Bind off loosely in pat.

Make 2nd glove same as first.

Finishing
Weave in ends. Block lightly. ※

MATERIALS
• 1 1oz/28g ball (approx
218yds/199m) of *Windy
Valley Qiviut Luxury Blend,*
45% qiviut/45% merino
wool/10% silk, in #2005 rust
• Size 1 (2.5mm) double-
pointed needles (dpns),
OR SIZE NEEDED TO
OBTAIN GAUGE
• Stitch markers
• Waste yarn
• Tapestry needle

**Some lucky
angler will have
warm hands next
fishing trip.**

Boyfriend Scarf

MATERIALS

1. Urban Scarf
• 2 4oz/113g hanks (each approx 190yds/174m) of *Lorna's Laces Bullfrogs and Butterflies*, 85% wool/15% mohair, each in #50ns poppy (A) and #9ns pewter (B)

2. Rainbow Coalition Scarf
• 1 3.5oz/100g skein (each approx 210yds/193m) of *Berroco, Inc. Comfort*, 50% superfine nylon/50% superfine acrylic, each in #9750 primary red (A), #9731 kidz orange (B), #9732 primary yellow (C), #9740 seedling (D), #9735 delft blue (E), #9737 aster (F), #9722 purple (G)

3. Hunter Scarf
• 5 1.75oz/50g hanks (each approx 98yds/90m) of *Berroco, Inc. Jasper*, 100% fine merino wool, in #3810 copper silk
• Size 9 (5.5mm) needles, OR SIZE NEEDED TO OBTAIN GAUGE

BEGINNER

Sizes
Scarves 1 and 2 Approx 12" x 66"/30.5 x 167.5cm
Scarf 3 12" x 90"/30.5 x 228.5cm (without fringe)

Gauge
18 sts and 24 rows = 4"/10cm in St st
TAKE TIME TO CHECK GAUGE

1. Urban Scarf
With A, cast on 56 sts.
Scarf with fringe K 4 rows, work Rows 1 and 2 from Rainbow Coalition Scarf.
Scarf without fringe Work same as Rainbow Coalition Scarf through Row 2.

Work both versions as follows:
Work in St st with A for 17"/43cm. Change to B.
Work in St st with B for 54"/137cm. Change to A.
Work in St st with A for 17"/43cm.
Work drop st row from Rainbow Coalition Scarf.

Scarf with fringe K 4 rows, then bind off.
Scarf without fringe Work in Garter st for 1"/2.5cm, then bind off.
Unravel columns of sts from dropped st to beg garter edge.

Fringe (make 12)
For each fringe, cut 15 strands of A 17"/43cm long. Fold in half, insert loop end through first drop st at end of scarf and draw ends through loop. Rep for each drop st at both ends of scarf. Trim ends.

2. Rainbow Coalition Scarf
With A, cast on 56 sts. Work in Garter st for 1"/2.5cm.
Row 1 (RS) K5, *bind off 1 st, k8; rep from * to last 6 sts, bind off 1 st, k5.
Row 2 P5, *cast on 1 st, p8; rep from * to last 5 sts, cast on 1 st, p5.
Cont in St st, *work 26 rows each in A, B, C, D, E, F and G; rep from * once more.

Drop st row (RS) K5, *drop next st, cast on 1 st, k8; rep from * to last 6 sts, drop next st, cast on 1 st, k5.
Work in Garter st for 1"/2.5cm.
Bind off.
Unravel columns of sts from dropped st to beg garter edge.

3. Hunter Scarf
Cast on 56 sts.
Work same as Rainbow Coalition Scarf without color changes. ✳

In case you've got more than one boyfriend, I've created one pattern that accommodates three different color schemes. That way, Tom, Dick and Harry will never know another guy is wearing this "just for him" scarf.

Urban Scarf

Since scarves don't have to "fit," you
can use almost any of your favorite yarns
(of any weight) from your stash.

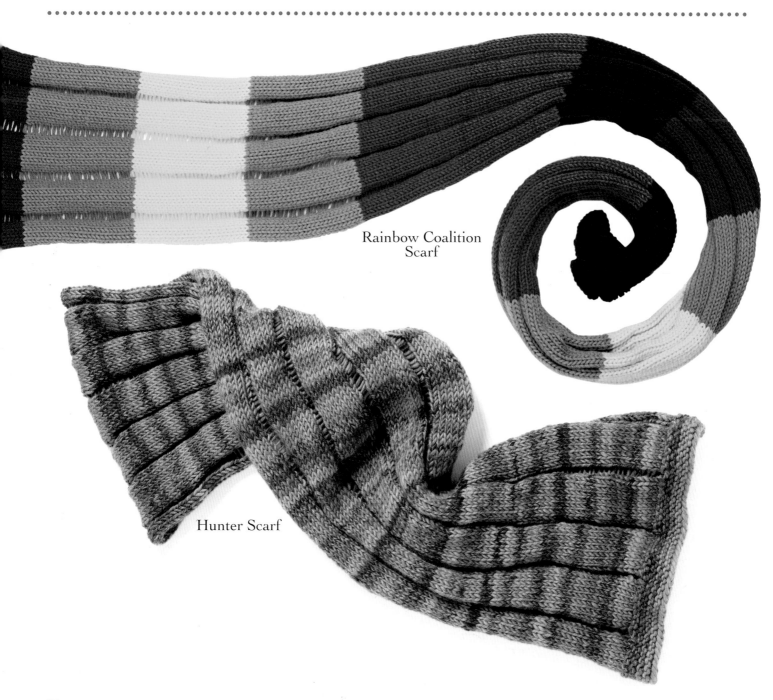

Rainbow Coalition
Scarf

Hunter Scarf

Bad Boy Socks

MATERIALS
- 1 1.75oz/50g hank (each approx 191yds/175m) of *Artyarns Ultramerino 4*, 100% merino wool, each in #249 tan (A), #246 black (B) and #244 red (C)
- Size 3 (3.25mm) double-pointed needles (dpns), OR SIZE NEEDED TO OBTAIN GAUGE
- Stitch marker
- Tapestry needle

Who doesn't love a bad boy? Yours will feel a kiss in every stitch with every step he takes. Good boys need not apply!

Finished measurements
9"/23cm from cuff to heel
Approx 11½"/29cm from heel to toe

Gauge
28 sts and 38 rows = 4"/10cm in St st
TAKE TIME TO CHECK GAUGE

Leg
With B, cast on 65 sts. Divide over 3 dpns, pm and join.

Rnds 1–10 With B, *k3, p2; rep from * to end.
Rnds 11–20 With A, rep Rnds 1–10.
Rnds 21–30 With C, rep Rnds 1–10.
Rnds 31–44 With B, [k3, p2] 3 times, k35, [k3, p2] 3 times.
Rnds 45–54 With A, rep Rnds 1–10.
Rnds 55–65 With C, rep Rnds 1–10.
Rnds 65–74 With B, rep Rnds 1–10.
Rnd 75 With C, rep Rnd 1.

Heel flap
Place last 16 sts of previous rnd on free needle, then remove marker and k 16.
Place rem 33 sts on hold for instep. Heel is worked over last 32 sts with C.
Row 1 (WS) Sl 1, p to end.
Row 2 *Sl 1, k1; rep from * to end.

Rep Rows 1 and 2 until 32 rows are complete, end with Row 2.

Turn heel
Row 1 (WS) Sl 1, p16, p2tog, p1. Turn.
Row 2 Sl 1, k3, ssk, k1. Turn.
Row 3 Sl 1, p to 1 st before gap, p2tog, p1. Turn.
Row 4 Sl 1, k to 1 st before gap, k2tog, k1. Turn.

Rep Rows 3 and 4 until there are 20 sts rem.
Rep Row 3 once more.
Next row Sl 1, k to1 st before gap, k2tog—18 sts.

Gussets
Cont with C and same needle (needle 1), pick up and k16 sts along side of heel; with needle 2, work in rib as est across 33 instep sts; with needle 3, pick up and k16 sts along other side of heel, k9 from needle 1—83 sts. Change to A.

Rnd 1 K to last 3 sts on needle 1, k2tog, k1; with needle 2, work in rib as est; with needle 3, k1, ssk, k to end.

You can add your own sentiment instead of "Bad Boy" to personalize your gift. Try a name or an initial.

Rnd 2 With needle 1, knit; with needle 2, work in rib as est; with needle 3, knit. Rep Rnds 1 and 2 until 65 sts rem.

Foot

Work even in pats as est until foot measures 8½"/21.5cm or 3"/7.5cm less than desired finished length.

Toe

Rnds 1–6 With A, knit.
Rnds 7–10 With B, knit.
Rnd 11 With C, knit, dec 1 st at center of needle 2—64 sts.
Rnd 12 K to last 3 sts on needle 1, k2tog, k1; k1, ssk, k to last 3 sts on needle 2, k2tog, k1; with needle 3, k1, ssk, k to end.
Rnd 13 Knit.

Rep Rnds 12 and 13 until 16 sts rem.
With needle 3, k4 from needle 1.
Graft toe sts.

Using duplicate st and C, embroider Bad Boy on St st section of Rnds 31–44 of leg. ❊

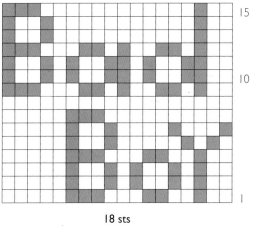

18 sts

CHART KEY

☐ B

▨ C

Gentry Lap Throw

EASY

Finished measurements
Approx 30" × 26"/76 × 66cm

Gauge
17 sts and 22 rows = 4"/10cm in k2, p2 rib, lightly blocked
TAKE TIME TO CHECK GAUGE

Button flap (make 10)
Cast on 10 sts.
Row 1 K2, *p2, k2; rep from * to end.
Row 2 P2, *k2, p2; rep from * to end.
Rep Rows 1 and 2 for 4"/10cm.
Break yarn and leave sts on needle. On same needle, cast on and work as above until 10 flaps are on the needle—do not break yarn after last flap.

Joining row *Work 10 sts of one flap, cast on 2 sts; rep from * to last flap, work 10 sts of last flap—118 sts.
Work in k2, p2 rib as est for 32"/81cm.
Work 6 rows in Garter st.
Bind off. Block lightly.

• **make it special tip**
Use decorative buttons to personalize this gift for anyone (even kids).

Pocket
Cast on 22 sts. Work Rows 1 and 2 of button flap for 6½"/16.5cm.
Bind off. Block lightly.

Place pocket on angle approx 15"/38cm from bottom edge and sew in place.

Finishing
Fold top 6"/15cm of flap edge to RS and sew one button to each flap to secure. Sew one button onto pocket. ✿

Grandpa or Grandma will love the warmth and sophistication of this throw that even has its own pocket. Or knit this for USA Cares' Operation Lap Wrap for a veteran in need (see page 120).

Serious Skull Cap

MATERIALS
- 1 50g ball each (each approx 135yds/123m) of *Lane Borgosesia/Trendsetter Yarns Merino 6-ply*, 100% wool in #11 black (A) and #1 white (B)
- Size 6 (4mm) needles, OR SIZE NEEDED TO OBTAIN GAUGE
- Size 5 (3.75mm) needles
- Tapestry needle

INTERMEDIATE

One size
Approx circumference 19"/48cm
Approx depth 9½"/24cm

Gauge
20 sts and 28 rows = 4"/10cm in St st using larger needles
TAKE TIME TO CHECK GAUGE

NOTE Instructions are given for chart pats to be worked in intarsia. Chart pats can also be worked in duplicate st. if desired.

Cap
With A and smaller needles, cast on 100 sts. Work in St st for 1"/2.5cm, end with a RS row. K 1 WS row for turning ridge. Change to larger needles. K 1 row, p 1 row.

Next row K2, work chart A over next 44 sts, k8, work chart B over next 44 sts, k2.
Cont in St st working rem 58 rows of chart.

Crown shaping
Row 1 (RS) *K2tog, k8; rep from * to end—90 sts.
Row 2 and all WS rows Purl.
Row 3 *K2tog, k7; rep from * to end—80 sts.
Row 5 *K2tog, k6; rep from * to end—70 sts.
Row 7 *K2tog, k5; rep from * to end—60 sts.
Row 9 *K2tog, k4; rep from * to end—50 sts.
Row 11 *K2tog, k3; rep from * to end—40 sts.
Row 13 *K2tog, k2; rep from * to end—30 sts.
Row 15 *K2tog, k1; rep from * to end—20 sts.
Row 17 *K2tog; rep from * to end—10 sts.

Break yarn and thread tail through rem sts. Pull tight to gather and secure.

Sew back seam. Fold hem to inside of hat at turning ridge and sew in place. ❈

Seriously worked in intarsia using two colors, this hat features a popular icon — the skull.

*Your skull doesn't have
to be white—for a girl, pink
would be hot.*

Skull Cap Chart 1   Skull Cap Chart 2

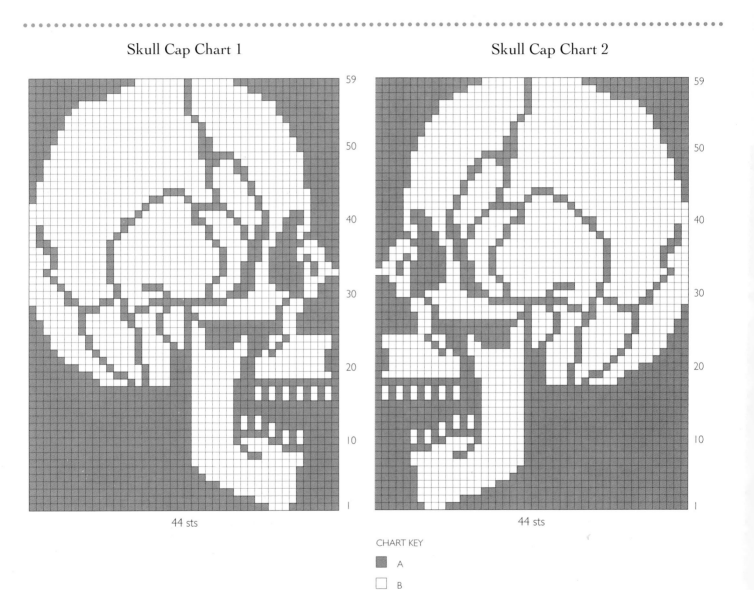

44 sts   44 sts

CHART KEY

A

B

chapter four
special friends

A Charitable Gift Afghan

MATERIALS
- 3 3.5oz/100g hanks (each approx 220yds/201m) of *Cascade Yarns 220 Superwash,* 100% wool, in #910A off white (A)
- 4 hanks #1913 dk grey (D)
- 2 hanks each in #892 lt grey (B), #900 heather grey (C), #836 lt pink (E) and #893 red (G)
- 1 hank in #901 med pink (F)
- Size 7 (4.5mm) needles (straight and dpns)
- Size 8 (5mm) circular needle, 40" (102cm long) OR SIZE TO OBTAIN GAUGE
- Size 9 (5.5mm) needles
- Size G-6 (4mm) crochet hook
- Tapestry needle
- Cable needle (cn)

INTERMEDIATE

Finished measurements
Approx 51½" x 61"/132 x 155cm
Each block measures 9½"/24cm square

Gauge
20 sts and 24 rows = 4"/10cm in St st on size 8 (5mm) needles
TAKE TIME TO CHECK GAUGE

Special abbreviations
4-st LC Sl 2 sts to cn and hold to *front,* k2, k2 from cn.
4-st RC Sl 2 sts to cn and hold to *back,* k2, k2 from cn.
ssp Sl the next two sts purlwise, one at a time, to RH needle. Insert tip of LH needle into fronts of these sts from left to right and purl them tog.

Block I
Basketweave floral (make 3)
With A and size 8 (5mm) needles, cast on 44 sts. P1 row.
Rows 1, 3, 5 and 7 (RS) K2, *k6, [p1, k1] twice; rep from * to last 2 sts, k2.
Rows 2, 4, 6 and 8 K2, *[k1, p1] twice, k1, p5; rep from * to last 2 sts, k2.
Rows 9, 11, 13 and 15 K2, *[k1, p1] twice, k6; rep from * to last 2 sts, k2.
Rows 10, 12, 14 and 16 K2, *p5, [k1, p1] twice, k1; rep from * to last 2 sts, k2.
Rep Rows 1–16 three times more. P 1 row. Bind off.

Flower (make 9)
With E and size 8 (5mm) needles, cast on 4 sts.
Row 1 (WS) K1, yo, k2, yo, k1—6 sts.
Rows 2 and 4 Knit.
Row 3 K2, yo, k2tog, yo, k2—7sts.
Row 5 K3, yo, k2tog, yo, k2—8 sts.
Row 6 Bind off 4 sts, k to end—4 sts.
Rep Rows 1–6 six times more, binding off all 8 sts in last row.
Thread tail through stitches along straight edge, pull tightly to gather and secure. Sew seam. Sew 3 flowers to each block as pictured.

Bobble (make 9)
With F and size 8 (5mm) needles, cast on 1 st.
Row 1 (RS) K in front, back, front, back, front of st—5 sts.
Rows 2 and 4 Purl.
Row 3 Knit.
Row 5 K2tog, k1, k2tog—3 sts.
Row 6 P3tog.
Fasten off. Using tails, sew one to center of each flower.

Block II
Bow stitch (make 3)
With E and size 8 (5mm) needles, cast on 37 sts. K1 row, p1 row.
Rows 1, 3 and 5 K6, *wyif sl next 5 sts, k5; rep from * to last st, k1.
Row 2 and all WS rows Purl.
Row 7 K8, *insert needle under the 3 loose strands, yarn over needle and draw up a loop, k next st and slip loop over this st, k9; rep from * to last 9 sts, insert needle under the 3 loose strands,

Here's a perfect group project to brighten anyone's day. Spread the joy and split up the blocks among your friends, and you'll have a truly cherished gift for someone special in no time at all.

Personalize this gift with letters—as names, initials or warm wishes—to make it a truly memorable gift.

yarn over needle and draw up a loop, k next st and slip loop over this st, k8.

Rows 9, 11 and 13 K1, *wyif sl next 5 sts, k5; rep from * to last 6 sts, wyif sl next 5 sts, k1.

Row 15 K3, *insert needle under the 3 loose strands, yarn over needle and draw up a loop, k next st and slip loop over this st, k9; rep from * to last 4 sts, insert needle under the 3 loose strands, yarn over needle and draw up a loop, k next st and slip loop over this st, k3.

Row 16 Purl.

Rep Rows 1–16 three times more.

Next row Knit.

Bind off knitwise.

Block III
Holding hands (make 3)

With F and size 8 (5mm) needles, cast on 42 sts. K 1 row, p 1 row.

Rows 1, 3 and 5 (RS) P3, *k4, p4; rep from * to last 7 sts, k4, p3.

Rows 2 and 4 Purl.

Row 6 P3, *k4, p4; rep from * to last 7 sts, k4, p3.

Row 7 P1, *4-st LC, 4-st RC; rep from * to last st, p1.

Row 8 Purl.

Rep Rows 1–8 five times more. K1 row. Bind off purlwise.

Block IV
Cables and bars (make 3)

With C and size 9 (5.5mm) needles, cast on 50 sts. K 1 row.

Rows 1, 3, and 5 (WS) K3, *p4, k2, p2, k2; rep from * to last 7 sts, p4, k3.

Row 2 P3, *4-st LC, p2, wyib insert needle purlwise through next st and k second st, then k first st tbl and drop both sts from LH needle—twist st, p2; rep from * to last 7 sts, 4-st LC, p3.

Rows 4 and 6 P3, *k4, p2, work twist st over next 2 sts, p2; rep from * to last 7 sts, k4, p3.

Rep Rows 1–6 nine times more.

Bind off in pattern.

Block V
Kiss stitch (make 3)

With G and size 7 (4.5mm) needles, cast on 47 sts.

Row 1 (RS) K10, *p9, k9; rep from * to last st, k1.

Row 2 P10, *k9, p9; rep from * to last st, p1.

Rows 3 and 5 Knit.

Rows 4 and 6 Purl.

Rows 7 and 8 Rep Rows 1 and 2.

Row 9 K14, *insert needle in front of next st in Row 1 and draw up a loop, slip loop onto left-hand needle and knit tog with next st, k17; rep from *, end last rep k14.

Row 10 Purl.

Row 11 K1, *p9, k9; rep from * to last 10 sts, p9, k1.

Row 12 P1, *k9, p9; rep from * to last 10 sts, k9, p1.

Rows 13 and 15 Knit.

Rows 14 and 16 Purl.

Rows 17 and 18 Rep Rows 11 and 12.

Row 19 K5, *insert needle in front of next st in Row 11 and draw up a loop, slip loop onto left-hand needle and knit tog with next st, k17; rep from *, end last rep k5.

Row 20 Purl.

Rep Rows 1–20 twice more.

Block VI
Hourglass lace (make 3)

With B and size 7 (4.5mm) needles, cast on 46 sts. K 1 row, p 1 row.

Row 1 (RS) K4, *k2tog, yo, k5; rep from * to end.

Row 2 P3, *ssp, yo, p1, yo, p2tog, p2; rep from * to last st, p1.

Row 3 K2, *k2tog, yo, k3, yo, ssk; rep from * to last 2 sts, k2.

Row 4 Purl.

Row 5 K2, *yo, ssk, k5; rep from * to last 2 sts, yo, ssk.

Row 6 P2, *yo, p2tog, p2, ssp, yo, p1; rep from * to last 2 sts, p2.

Row 7 K4, *yo, ssk, k2tog, yo, k3;

rep from * to end.

Row 8 Purl.

Rep rows 1–8 six times more. K 1 row, p 1 row.

Bind off.

Block VII
All hearts (make 3)

With G and size 7 (4.5mm) needles, cast on 41 sts. K 1 row, p 1 row.

Row 1 (RS) K3, *yo, k2tog, k3, yo, k1, yo, k3, ssk, yo, k1; rep from * to last 2 sts, k2—47 sts.

Row 2 and all WS rows Purl.

Row 3 K3, *k1, yo, k4tog, yo, k3, yo, ssssk (sl next 4 sts knitwise, one at a time, to RH needle, insert LH needle into fronts of these 4 sts and k them tog tbl), yo, k2; rep from * to last 2 sts, k2—41 sts.

Row 5 K3, *k1, k2tog, yo, k5, yo, ssk, k2; rep from * to last 2 sts, k2.

Row 7 K3, *k2tog, yo, k7, yo, ssk, k1; rep from * to last 2 sts, k2.

Row 9 K2, k2tog, *yo, k9, yo, sk2p; rep from * to last 13 sts, yo, k9, yo, ssk, k2.

Row 10 Purl.

Rep Rows 1–10 five times more. K 1 row, p 1 row.

Bind off.

Block VIII
Breast cancer/AIDS emblem (make 3)

With A and size 8 (5mm) needles, cast on 45 sts. K 1 row, p 1 row.

Row 1 K1, *p1, k1; rep from * to end.

Rep Row 1 for 8"/20.5cm, end with a WS row. K 1 row, p 1 row.

Bind off.

Emblem
(make 3—one in G, 2 in F)

With size 7 (5mm) dpns, cast on 5 sts. Work in I-cord (see page 123) for 12"/30.5cm. Bind off. Pin to block as pictured and sew in place.

You'll need a total of 30 blocks.
Any of the 8 blocks can be repeated or
omitted, so feel free to be creative.

Block IX Striped with Heart

Block X Lettering

Block IX
Striped with heart (make 3)
With A and size 8 (5mm) needles,
cast on 41 sts.
With A, work in St st for 18 rows.
With D, work in St st for 18 rows.
With E, work in St st for 18 rows.
Bind off.

Heart (make 3)
With G and size 8 (5mm) needles, cast on 3
sts. With a separate ball of yarn, cast 3 more
sts onto same needle—6 sts.
Row 1 (RS) *[K1, m1] twice, k1; rep on second
set of sts—5 sts each set.
Row 2 and all WS rows Purl.
Row 3 *K1, m1, k to last st, m1, k1; rep on
second set of sts—7 sts each set.
Row 5 and 7 Rep Row 3—11 sts each set
after Row 7.
Row 9 (joining row) *K1, m1, k9, k2tog, k9,
m1, k1—23 sts. Cut second yarn.
Row 11 Knit.
Row 13 and all RS rows through Row 29
K1, ssk, k to last 3 sts, k2tog, k1—5 sts after
Row 29.
Row 31 K1, sk2p, k1—3 sts.
Row 33 Sk2p—1 st.
Fasten off.
Pin to block as pictured and sew in place.

Block X
Lettering (make 3)
With B and size 8 (5mm) needles,
cast on 41 sts.
Work in St st for 55 rows. Bind off.
Using A (or your color choice), duplicate-stitch
lettering following charts for LOVE, HOPE
and/or a name (I chose ANNE). With D,
duplicate-stitch embellishments above and
below lettering.

Finishing
Edging
NOTE: Use colors to correspond with each
block, changing colors on Block IX as needed.
With RS facing and crochet hook, starting at
upper left corner, work 3 sc in corner, sc
evenly across edge to next corner (taking care
to keep block flat and work the same number
across each edge); rep from * to end. Join with
sl st in first sc. Fasten off.

Work a second row with D. Fasten off.
Work edging for each block using the same
number of sc sts.
Block each piece to 9½"/25cm square. Arrange
30 blocks, alternating patterns as desired. With
WS facing, D and crochet hook, join blocks
using sl st working in top loops only.

Border
Working one edge at a time, with RS facing, D
and size 8 (5mm) needles, pick up and knit
200 sts across top and bottom edges and 240
along each side edge.
Row 1 (WS) Knit.
Row 2 K in front and back of first st, k to last
st, k in front and back of last st.
Rep Rows 1 and 2 for 2"/5cm. Bind off.
Sew corner seams.
Block afghan to measurements. ❋

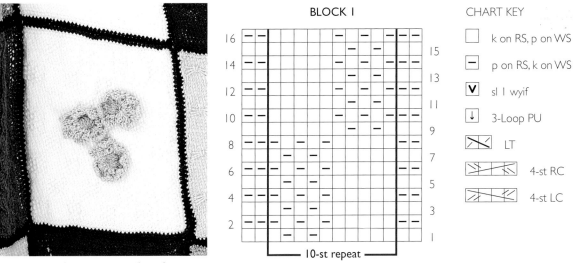

BLOCK 1

16
14
12
10
8
6
4
2

15
13
11
9
7
5
3
1

10-st repeat

Block I Basketweave Floral

CHART KEY

☐ k on RS, p on WS

— p on RS, k on WS

Ⅴ sl 1 wyif

↓ 3-Loop PU

◢ LT

◢◢ 4-st RC

◢◢ 4-st LC

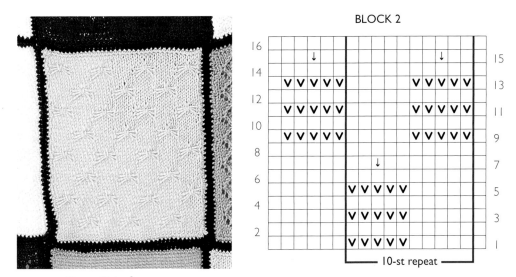

BLOCK 2

16
14
12
10
8
6
4
2

15
13
11
9
7
5
3
1

10-st repeat

Block II Bow Stitch

BLOCK 3

8
6
4
2

7
5
3
1

8-st repeat

BLOCK 4

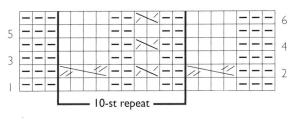

5
3
1

6
4
2

10-st repeat

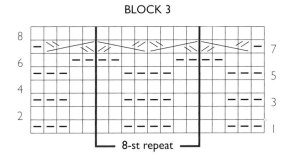

BLOCK 5

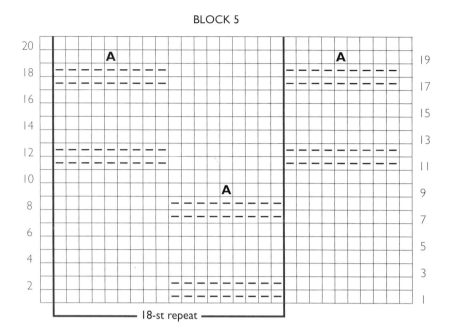

18-st repeat

BLOCK 6

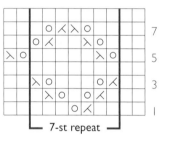

7-st repeat

CHART KEY

□	k on RS, p on WS	○ yo
−	p on RS, k on WS	⊿ k4tog
⟋	k2tog on RS, p2tog on WS	⊾ ssssk
⟍	ssk on RS, ssp on WS	⋏ S2KP
		▣ no stitch
		A make loop

BLOCK 7

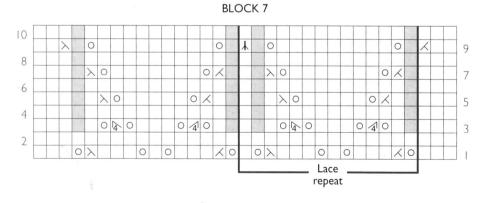

Lace repeat

Block V Kiss Stitch

Block VI Hourglass Lace

Block VII All Hearts

Charity Afghan Alphabet

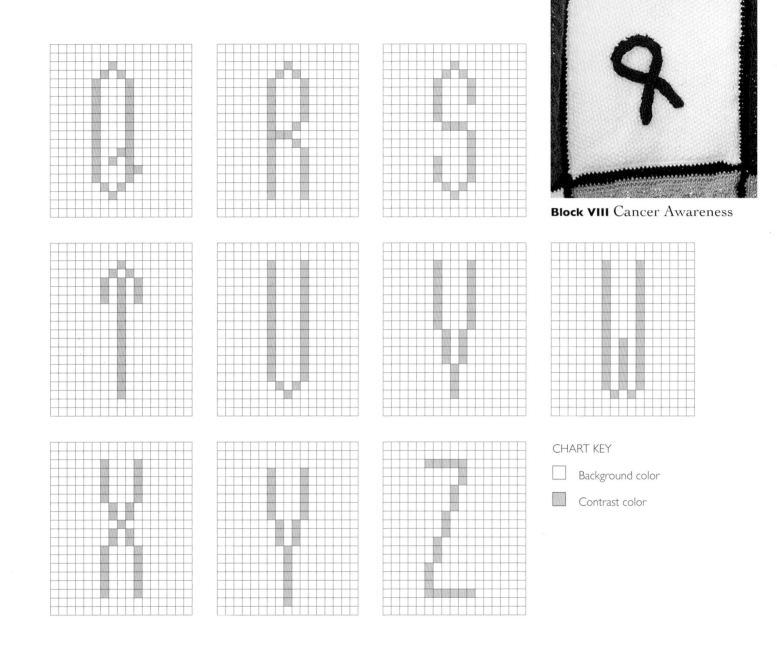

Block VIII Cancer Awareness

CHART KEY

☐ Background color

▨ Contrast color

I have included an alphabet so the afghan can be customized
with names or initials or a warm sentiment.

Family Footies

MATERIALS

1. Man's
- 1 2oz/55g hank (approx 400yds/366m) of *Jade Sapphire Mongolian Cashmere 2ply*, 100% Mongolian cashmere, in #50 driftwood (A)

2. Woman's and child's
- 2 1.75oz/50g hank (each approx 160yds/146m) of *Artyarns Cashmere Sock*, 67% cashmere/25% wool/8% nylon, in #168 baby (B)
NOTE This is enough for both pairs unless making larger sizes.
- Size 3 (3.25mm) needles, OR SIZE TO OBTAIN GAUGE
- Size 2 (2.75mm) double-pointed needles (dpns)
- Stitch marker
- Size 8 (1.25mm) crochet hook
- 64 (40) pearl seed beads (size 6/0)
- Tapestry needle

EASY

Sizes
Man's (Woman's Child's)

Finished measurements
Approx 9 (8, 5)"/23 (20.5, 13)cm foot circumference
Approx 10¾ (9¼, 5½)"/ 27.5 (23.5, 14)cm from heel to toe

Gauge
32 sts and 46 rows = 4"/10cm in St st with A using larger needles
32 sts and 42 rows = 4"/10cm in St st with B using larger needles
TAKE TIME TO CHECK GAUGE

Special abbreviation
AB (Add Bead) Pick up bead with crochet hook, then pick up stitch from left-hand needle and pull through bead. Return beaded stitch to left-hand needle and knit the stitch.

Cuff
With smaller needles and A (B, B), cast on 72 (64, 40) sts. Divide sts evenly over 3 needles as follows: needles 1 and 3—24 (20, 12); needle 2—24 (24, 16).

1. Man's sock
Rnds 1, 3 and 5 Purl.
Rnds 2, 4 and 6 Knit.
Rnds 7, 8 and 9 *K2, p2; rep from *.

2. Woman's and child's socks
Rnds 1, 3 and 5 *K2, p2; rep from *.
Rnd 2 *K1, AB, p2; rep from *.
Rnd 4 *AB, k1, p2; rep from *.

ALL SIZES
Change to larger needles and k 1 rnd.
K36 (32, 20) heel sts and distribute rem 36 (32, 20) sts evenly over 2 needles for instep to be worked later.

What says love more than cashmere? If you've got loved ones with cold feet, you'll warm them with these cozy, soft socks. Best of all, they're sized for the whole family.

You can make a child's pair with
the yarn you have left over from the
two hanks used for one adult pair.

Heel

Heel flap is worked back and forth
over 36 (32, 20) sts.
Row 1 Sl 1, p to end.
Row 2 *Sl 1, k1; rep from * to end.
Rep Rows 1 and 2 until there are 36 (32, 20)
rows in heel flap.
TURN HEEL
Row 1 (WS) Sl 1, p18 (16, 10), p2tog,
p1, turn.

Row 2 Sl 1, k3, ssk, k1, turn.
Row 3 Sl 1, p to 1 st before gap, p2tog,
p1, turn.
Row 4 Sl 1, k to 1 st before gap, ssk,
k1, turn.
Rep Rows 3 and 4 until all heel sts have been
worked—20 (18, 12) sts.

Gusset

With same needle (needle 1), pick up and k18
(16, 10) sts along side of heel;
with needle 2, k36 (32, 20) instep sts;
with needle 3, pick up and k18 (16, 10) sts
along other side of heel, k10 (9, 6) from
needle 1—92 (82, 52) sts. Pm for end of rnd.

SHAPE GUSSETS
Rnd 1 Knit.
Rnd 2 For needle 1, k to last 3 sts, k2tog, k1;
for needle 2, knit; for needle 3, k1, ssk,
k to end.
Rep Rnds 1 and 2 until there are 72
(64, 40) sts.

Foot

Work in St st until foot measures
8¼ (7, 4¼)"/21 (18, 11)cm long or 2½ (2¼,
1¼)"/6.5 (6, 3)cm less than desired length.

Toe

Rnd 1 Knit.
Rnd 2 For needle 1, k to last 3 sts, k2tog, k1;
for needle 2, k1, ssk, k to last 3 sts, k2tog, k1;
for needle 3, K1, ssk, k to end.
Rep Rnds 1 and 2 until there are 16 sts.
With needle 3, k4 from needle 1.
Graft toe sts using Kitchener st
(see page 124). ※

To: PAPA, MAMA
+ BABY BEAR
From:
WITH LOVE,
Nicky

Pampering Spa Cloths

MATERIALS
- 1 3oz/85g ball (each approx 103yds/94m) of *Lion Brand Yarn Nature's Choice Organic Cotton,* 100% cotton, each in #99 macadamia (A), #170 pistachio (B), #98 almond (C), #125 walnut (D), #101 strawberry (E) and #124 pecan (F)
- Size 9 (5.5mm) needles OR SIZE NEEDED TO OBTAIN GAUGE
- Size 7 (4.5mm) double-pointed needles (dpns)
- Tapestry needle

▨■☐☐
EASY

Finished measurements
Approx 10" x 11"/25.5 x 28cm each

Gauges
15 sts and 30 rows = 4"/10cm in Garter st on larger needles
13½ sts and 24 rows = 4"/10cm in Seed st on larger needles
TAKE TIME TO CHECK GAUGE

SPECIAL ABBREVIATION
Sp2p Slip 1 st knitwise, p2tog, pass slipped st over just made st.

1. Tea Leaf Cloth
With A, cast on 41 sts. Work in Garter st for 10"/25.5cm. Bind off.

LEAF
With B, cast on 11 sts.
Row 1 (RS) Knit.
Row 2 and all WS rows Purl.
Row 3 K1, m1, k9, m1, k1—13 sts.
Row 5 K1, m1, k11, m1, k1—15 sts.
Row 7 K1, m1, k13, m1, k1—17 sts.
Rows 9, 11 and 13 Knit.
Rows 15, 17, 19, 21, 23, 25 and 27 K2tog, k to last 2 sts, k2tog—3 sts after Row 27.
Row 29 Sk2p.
Fasten off.
Using A, embroider veins on leaf with Stem st. Sew leaf to cloth.

2. Tree Breeze Cloth
With C, work Garter st cloth same as cloth 1.

Tree
With dpns and D, cast on 4 sts. Work in I-cord (see page 123) for 4"/10cm, dec 1 st in last row—3 sts. Cont in I-cord for 5"/12.5cm. Fasten off. Referring to photo for branch placement, pick up and k3 sts for each I-cord branch along main trunk and branches. Sew tree to cloth. With B, embroider small leaf to tree as pictured.

3. Flower Blossom Cloth
With E, cast on 37 sts.
Row 1 *K1, p1; rep from *, end k1.
Rep Row 1 to continue in Seed st for 10"/25.5cm. Bind off.

FLOWER
With A, cast on 18 sts.
Row 1 Knit.
Row 2 Purl.
Row 3 K1, *m1, k1; rep from * to end—35 sts.
Rows 4–14 Work in St st.

RIGHT-SIDE PETAL
Row 15 K11. Turn, leaving rem sts on needle for center and left petals.
Rows 16, 18, 20, 22 and 24 Purl.
Row 17 K9, k2tog.
Row 19 K8, k2tog.
Row 21 K7, k2tog.
Row 23 Ssk, k4, k2tog—6 sts.
Row 25 Ssk, bind off 2 sts, k2tog, bind off rem sts.

Showering and bathing have never looked or felt so good.

Earthy, organic and green-friendly cloths will be a hit as housewarming gifts.

CENTER PETAL

With RS facing, attach yarn to center petal.
Row 15 K13. Turn, leaving rem sts on needle for left petal.
Rows 16, 18, 20 and 22 Purl.
Rows 17, 19 and 21 Ssk, k to last 2 sts, k2tog—7 sts after row 21.
Row 23 Ssk, bind off 2 sts, k2tog, bind of rem sts.

LEFT SIDE PETAL

With RS facing, attach yarn to left petal.
Row 15 K11.
Rows 16, 18, 20, 22 and 24 Purl.
Row 17 Ssk, k9.
Row 19 Ssk, k8.
Row 21 Ssk, k7.
Row 23 Ssk, k4, k2tog—6 sts.
Row 25 Ssk, bind off 2 sts, k2tog, bind off rem sts.

BOBBLES (MAKE 6)

With F, cast on 1 st.
Row 1 (RS) K in front, back, front, back, front of st—5 sts.
Rows 2 and 4 Purl.
Row 3 Knit.

Flower Blossom

Leafy Branch

Row 5 K2tog, k1, k2tog—3 sts.
Row 6 P3tog.
Fasten off.

Sew flower to lower right corner of cloth as pictured. Using tails, tie 6 bobbles to flower "center." To hide ends, thread bobble tails back into center of bobbles. Using F, embroider veins onto petals with Stem st.

4. Leafy Branch Cloth

With B, work Seed st cloth same as cloth 3.

BRANCH WITH LEAF

With dpns and F, cast on 3 sts. Work in I-cord for 8"/21cm, inc 2 sts on last row—5 sts.
Row 1 (WS) Purl.
Row 2 K2, yo, k1, yo, k2—7 sts.
Rows 3, 5, 7, 9, 11 and 13 Purl.
Row 4 K3, yo, k1, yo, k3—9 sts.
Row 6 K4, yo, k1, yo, k4—11 sts.
Row 8 Ssk, k7, k2tog—9 sts.
Row 10 Ssk, k5, k2tog—7 sts.
Row 12 Ssk, k3, k2tog—5 sts.
Row 14 Ssk, k1, k2tog—3 sts.

Tea Leaf

Tree Breeze

Row 15 Sp2p—1 st.
Fasten off.

LEAVES (MAKE 4)

With F, cast on 5 sts. Work Rows 1–15 of Leafy Branch. Fasten off.

Sew branch with leaf and 4 leaves to cloth as pictured. ✳

Kiss Me
Wrap-Around

MATERIALS
• 1 1.75oz/50g ball
(each approx 122yds/110m)
of *GGH/Muench Maxima,*
100% extra fine superwash
merino wool, each in
#15 lt pink (A and
#19 red (B)
• Size 5 (3.75mm) needles,
OR SIZE TO OBTAIN
GAUGE
• Size 5 (3.75mm) double-
pointed needles (dpns)
• Purchased microwaveable
neck warmer
• Five ½"/1.5cm buttons
• Tapestry needle

Finished measurements
Approx 9½" x 19"/24 x 48.5cm tube, buttoned

Gauge
20 sts and 28 rows = 4"/10cm in St st
TAKE TIME TO CHECK GAUGE

NOTE Lips are worked in duplicate st after
piece is knit.

With B, cast on 40 sts. Work in St st for 1½"/4cm,
end with a RS row.
Next row (WS) Knit.
Next row Knit for turning row.
Cont in St st for 1½"/4cm, end with a RS row.
Change to A and work in St st for 16"/40.5cm.
Change to B and work in St st for 1½"/4cm, end
with a RS row.
Next row (WS) Knit.
Next row Knit.
Continue in St st for 1½"/4cm. Bind off.

Finishing
With B, work 4 duplicate st lips, referring
to photo for placement.

Button band
With RS facing and B, pick up and k96 sts along
length of cover, excluding hems.
Row 1 (WS) *P3, k3; rep from * to end.
Row 2 *K3, p3; rep from * to end.
Rep Rows 1 and 2 for 1¼"/3cm. Bind off in rib.

Buttonhole band
Pick up same as for button band.
Row 1 (WS) *K3, p3; rep from * to end.
Rep Row 1 three times more.
Buttonhole row (WS) Rib 5, [bind off next 2 sts,
rib next 19 sts] 4 times, bind off 2 sts, rib to end.
Next row (RS) Work in rib, casting on 2 sts over
each bound-off space. Work even until same
length as button band.

Ties (make 2)
With B and dpns, cast on 4 sts. Work in I-cord
(see page 123) for 16"/40.5cm. Bind off.

Fold each end along turning row to WS for casing.
Sew in place on WS, keeping sides open, thread
ties through opening. ❈

Why knit a gift for a pain in the neck? Because it feels good!
This is a cover for those wonderful pain-relieving
microwaveable neck pads, to make the heat more comfortable.

Be sure to use a washable
yarn, or you might end up with a
felted neck pad.

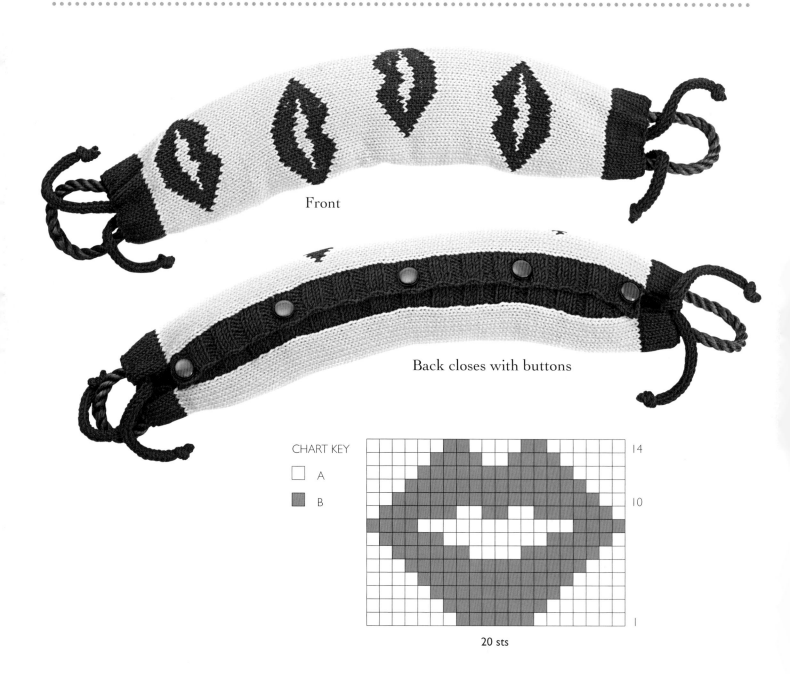

Front

Back closes with buttons

CHART KEY

☐ A

▨ B

14

10

1

20 sts

Sweet Socks

MATERIALS
- 2 2oz/56g skeins (each approx 215yds/197m) of *Lorna's Laces Shepherd Sock*, 80% superwash wool/20% nylon, in hope (for Rib Lace socks) or whisper (for Cable-and-Lace socks)
- Size 3 (3.25mm) straight needles (for Cable-and-Lace socks)
- Size 3 (3.25mm) double-pointed needles (dpns) (for Rib Lace socks), OR SIZE TO OBTAIN GAUGE
- Size 2 (2.75mm) double-pointed needles (dpns)
- Stitch marker
- Tapestry needle
- Cable needle

~~~~~~

These dainty lace-edge socks will put a smile on any big girl's face.

INTERMEDIATE

Finished measurements
6"/15cm from cuff to heel
Approx 9½"/24cm from heel to toe

Gauge
32 sts and 44 rows = 4"/10cm in St st using larger needles
TAKE TIME TO CHECK GAUGE

I. Rib Lace Socks
Pattern stitches
RIB LACE (MULTIPLE OF 5 STS)
Rnds 1 and 3 *K3, p2; rep from *.
Rnd 2 *K1, yo, ssk, p2; rep from *.
Rnd 4 *K2tog, yo, k1, p2; rep from *.
Rep Rnds 1–4 for pattern.

POINT EDGING (OVER 6 STS)
Rows 1, 3, 5 and 7 Sl 1, k1, m1, k2tog, M1, k to end—10 sts after Row 7.
Rows 2, 4 and 6 Sl 1, k to last 3 sts, m1, k2tog, k1.
Row 8 Bind off 4 sts, k2, m1, k2tog, k1—6 sts.
Rep Rows 1–8 for pattern.

Cuff
With larger dpns, cast on 60 sts. Divide evenly over 3 needles, pm and join.

Work in Rib lace pat for 2¼"/5.5cm, end with Rnd 1.

Change to smaller needles and work in k1, p1 rib for 1"/2.5cm.

Inc rnd Work in rib, inc 1 st at beg of first needle and at end of third needle.

Cont in rib as est, rep inc rnd every ½"/1cm once more—64 sts.

Cont even in rib until piece measures 5½"/14cm from beg.

Heel
Turn work inside out, W&T (see page 122) to work in opposite direction. Heel flap is worked back and forth over 32 sts.

K32 sts and distribute rem 32 sts evenly over 2 needles for instep to be worked later.
Row 1 Sl 1, p to end.
Row 2 (RS) *Sl 1, k1; rep from * to end.
Rep Rows 1 and 2 until there are 32 rows in heel flap, end with Row 2.

Turn heel
Row 1 (WS) Sl 1, p16, p2tog, p1, turn.
Row 2 Sl 1, k3, ssk, k1, turn.
Row 3 Sl 1, p to one st before gap, p2tog, p1, turn.
Row 4 Sl 1, k to one st before gap, k2tog, k1, turn.
Rep Rows 3 and 4 until all heel sts have been worked—18 sts.

Gussets
With RS facing, and cont with same needle (needle 1), pick up and k20 along side of heel flap; with needle 2, knit 32 instep sts; with needle 3, pick up and k20 along other side of heel flap, k9 from needle 1—90 sts. Pm for end of rnd.

SHAPE GUSSETS
Rnd 1 For needle 1, k to last 3 sts, k2tog, k1; for needle 2, knit; for needle 3, k1, ssk, k to end.
Rnd 2 Knit.
Rep Rnds 1 and 2 until there are 64 sts.

Foot
Work even in St st until foot measures 7½"/19cm or 2"/5cm less than desired length.

Using one color for the foot
and one color for the cuff is a cute
alternative idea.

CHART KEY

☐	k on RS, p on WS
⊟	p on RS, k on WS
◯	yo
⧄	k2tog
⧅	ssk
V	sl 1 purlwise
M	m1
⤡⤢	4-st LC
✕	bind-off

Rib Lace

Cable and Lace

CABLE & LACE

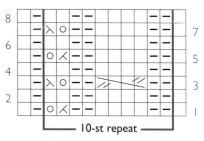

10-st repeat

RIB LACE

5-st repeat

POINT EDGING

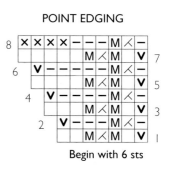

Begin with 6 sts

Toe

Rnd 1 Knit.
Rnd 2 For needle 1, k to last 3 sts, k2tog, k1; for needle 2, k1, ssk, k to last 3 sts, k2tog, k1; for needle 3, k1, ssk, k to end.
Rep Rnds 1 and 2 until there are 20 sts. With needle 3, k5 from Needle 1.

Graft toe sts using Kitchener st (see page 124).

Edging (make 2)

With larger needles, cast on 6 sts. Work Point edging to fit around cuff. Sew edging to each cuff. Sew seam of edging.❈

2. Cable-and-Lace Socks

Pattern stitches

CABLE AND LACE
(MULTIPLE OF 10 STS PLUS 3)
4-st LC Sl 2 sts to cn and hold to front, k2, k2 from cn.
Row 1 (RS) K1, *p2, k4, p2, k2tog, yo; rep from * to last 2 sts, p1, k1.

Row 2 and all WS rows P1, k1, *p2, k2, p4, k2; rep from * to last st, p1.
Row 3 K1, *p2, 4-st LC, p2, yo, ssk; rep from * to last 2 sts, p1, k1.
Row 5 Rep Row 1.
Row 7 K1, *p2, k4, p2, yo, ssk; rep from * to last 2 sts, p1, k1.
Row 8 Rep Row 2.
Rep Rows 1–8 for pattern.

Scalloped edging (multiple of 11 sts plus 2)

NOTE Stitch counts change in Rows 2 and 3.
Row 1 (RS) Purl.
Row 2 K2, *k1, sl this st back to LH needle, lift the next 8 sts on LH needle over this st and off needle, [yo] twice, k the first st on LH needle again, k2; rep from * across.
Row 3 K1, *p2tog, [k1, k1 tbl] twice into double yo, p1; rep from * to last st, k1.
Rows 4–8 Knit.
Bind off.

Cuff

With straight needles, cast on 83 sts.
Work back and forth in Cable and Lace pat for 2"/5cm, end with row 4.
Dec row P2tog, p1, *[k2tog] twice, p2, k2, p2; rep from * to end—62 sts.
Change to smaller needles. Pm and join. Work in k2, p2 rib until piece measures 5½"/14cm, inc 2 sts evenly around on last rnd—64 sts.

Work remainder of sock as for Rib and Lace Socks.

Edging (make 2)

With larger needles, cast on 101 sts. Work Rows 1–8 of Scalloped edging. Sew edging to each cuff. Sew back seam of edging and cuff.❈

Knitty Kitty Play Mat

MATERIALS

Mat
• 1 8oz/228g skein (each approx 130yds/119m) of *Brown Sheep Co. Burley Spun*, 100% wool, each in #181 prairie fire (A) and #4 charcoal heather (B)
• Size 19 (15mm) needles
• Size 13 (9mm) double-pointed needles (dpns)
• Tapestry needle

Mouse
Small amount of worsted-weight gray or black yarn
• Size 9 (5.5mm) needles
• Fiberfill

Kitties love to play with or sleep on this felted play mat. It's fun for your cat and saves wear and tear on your rugs.

EASY

Finished measurements
Approx 20" x 21"/51 x 53.5cm, before felting
Approx 15" x 19"/38 x 48.5cm, after felting

Gauge
7 sts and 14 rows = 4"/10cm in Garter st using larger needles

Cat Mat
Head
With A and larger needles, cast on 20 sts.
K 2 rows.
Inc row Kfb, k to last st, kfb.
Rep inc row every other row until there are 34 sts.
Work even in Garter st for 10"/25.5cm, end with a WS row.
Dec row Ssk, k to last 2 sts, k2tog.
Rep dec row every other row until 20 sts rem.
Bind off.

Ears (make 2)
With RS facing, larger needles and A, pick up and k17 sts along an upper diagonal edge. K 2 rows.
Rep dec row every other row until 3 sts rem.
Sk2p. Fasten off.

Nose
With B and larger needles, cast on 11 sts.
K 2 rows. Rep dec row every other row until 3 sts rem. Sk2p. Fasten off.

Inner ears (make 2)
Work same as nose.

Eyes (make 2)
With dpns and B, cast on 4 sts. Work I-cord (see page 123) for 7"/18cm. Pass 2nd, 3rd and 4th sts over first st. Fasten off.

Mouth
With dpns and B, cast on 3 sts. Work I-cord for 18"/45.5cm. Sk2p. Fasten off.

Mouse
Tail
Cast on 3 sts. Work I-cord for 5"/12.5cm.
Row 1 (RS) Yo, *k1, m1; rep from * to end—7 sts.
Rows 2 and 4 Purl.
Row 3 Rep Row 1—15 sts.
Row 5 K2, *[m1, k1] twice, k1, m1, k2; rep from * once more, [m1, k1] twice, k1—23 sts.
Cont in St st for 3"/7.5cm, end with a WS row.

SHAPE HEAD
Row 1 (RS) K5, s2kp, k7, s2kp, k5—19 sts.
Rows 2, 4, 6 and 8 Purl.
Row 3 K4, s2kp, k5, s2kp, k4—15 sts.
Row 5 K3, s2kp, k3, s2kp, k3—11 sts.
Row 7 K2, s2kp, k1, s2kp, k2—7 sts.
Row 9 K2, s2kp, k2—5 sts.

You can felt the mat or leave it unfelted. Choose your cat's favorite colors!

Cut yarn, leaving a long tail. Thread tail through rem sts, pull tightly and secure. Sew seam part way, stuff with fiberfill and sew closed.

Ears (make 2)
Cast on 5 sts.
Row 1 (RS) Knit.
Row 2 Purl.
Row 3 K1, s2kp, k1—3 sts.
Row 4 P3tog—1 st.
Fasten off.

Sew ears to sides of head at beginning of head shaping. Felt mouse following felting instructions. With black yarn, make French knots* for eyes.

Finishing
Sew all pieces to kitty face using photo as guide. Embroider whiskers using Stem st*.

Felt mat (see right). When pieces are dry, sew French knots* on mouse for eyes. Sew mouse to mat. ※

* see embroidery stitches on page 125.

• felting furry friends
1 Fill washing machine to low water setting at a hot temperature. Add ½ cup of gentle detergent.
2 Add all pieces (may be placed in a lingerie bag or pillowcase) and a pair of jeans or old towels to provide abrasion and balanced agitation. (**NOTE** yarn colors may bleed.)
3 Use 15–20 minute wash cycle, including cold rinse and spin. Repeat process until desired felting effect is achieved.
4 Lay flat to dry.

Before felting

More mice = more fun!

Barkley's Hat Scarf

MATERIALS
- 1 3.5oz/100g hank (each approx 174yds/160m) of *Berroco, Inc. Peruvia,* 100% Peruvian highland wool, each in #7127 palomino blue (A) and #7150 teal green (B)
- Size 10 (6mm) 16"/40cm circular needle, OR SIZE NEEDED TO OBTAIN GAUGE
- Tapestry needle
- Stitch holders
- Plastic for visor

Man's best friend will be warm and winsome in this all-in-one scarf and ear warmer.
If the ears don't fit, they still make a delightful topper for the ensemble.

Sizes
Small (Medium, Large) dog

Finished measurements
Approx 8½ (13, 16)"/21.5 (33, 40.5)cm circumference

Gauge
17 sts and 21 rows = 4"/10cm in St st
TAKE TIME TO CHECK GAUGE

Scarf (make two)
With A, cast on 18 (28, 34) sts.
Work 10 (14, 14) rows in St st, beg with a k row.
With B, work 8 (12, 12) rows in St st.
With A, work 10 (14, 14) rows in St st.
With B, work 8 (12, 12) rows in St st.
With A, work 34 (54, 74) rows in St st. Place sts on holder and work second piece.

Cap
Place 18 (28, 34), 36 (56, 68) sts of both pieces on circular needle with RS facing. Pm and join for working in rounds. With B, work in St st for 1 (1½, 2½)"/2.5 (4, 6.5)cm. Divide sts as follows: K13 (21, 25) and place on holder for right ear; k6 (8, 10) and place on holder for back; k13 (21, 25) and place on holder for left ear; k4 (6, 8) for front.

Front
Working back and forth, cont in St st for 6 (10, 12) rows.
Inc row Kfb, k2 (4, 6), kfb—6 (8, 10) sts.
Cont in St st for 10 (16, 20) rows with WS tog. Join with 6 (8, 10) back sts using 3-needle bind-off.

Ears
With RS facing, place 13 (21, 25) sts of one ear onto needle and attach B.
Row 1 (RS) K1, ssk, k to last 3 sts, k2tog, k1.
Row 2 Purl.

Rep Rows 1 and 2 until 5 sts rem.
Next row K1, s2kp, k1.
Next row P3 tog.
Fasten off.

With RS facing and B, pick up and k13 (21, 25) sts along edge of center band. P 1 row and rep from Row 1. Sew edges of ear closed.
Repeat for other side.

Visor
With A, cast on 17 (23, 25) sts. Work in St st for 3 (4, 4½)"/7.5 (10, 11.5)cm. Bind off.
Cut plastic for visor to 1½, (2, 2¼)" deep, with flat edge just under 4 (4½, 5)" wide. Cut curved edge as desired and cover. Center visor at front of cap and sides of scarf and sew in place.

Fringe
For each fringe, cut 3 strands of A 11"/30cm in length. Fold in half, insert loop end through end of scarf and draw ends through loop. Rep across both ends of scarf. Trim ends. ✳

Jet Set Travel Tags

MATERIALS
- Favorite yarns and needles—use your leftovers!
- Stitch holders
- Tapestry needle
- Glue (optional)

Autumn Leaf…
Corkscrew
Trio…Blooming
Flower: The perfect
gift for the jet-setter
in your life. These
personal luggage
tags will make life
easier at the baggage
claim area.

EASY

1. Flower power
Cast on 6 sts.
Row 1 (RS) K3, yo, k3—7 sts.
Rows 2, 4, 6, 8, 10 and all WS rows Knit.
Row 3 K3, yo, k4—8 sts.
Row 5 K3, yo, k5—9 sts.
Row 7 K3, yo, k6—10 sts.
Row 9 K3, yo, k7—11 sts.
Row 11 K3, yo, k8—12 sts.
Row 12 Bind off 6 sts, k to end—6 sts.
Rep Rows 1–12 four times more.
Bind off. Sew cast-on edge to bound-off edge to form a ring. Weave a length of yarn through eyelets and pull tight to gather. Secure ends.

Bobble
Cast on 1 st.
Row 1 (RS) K in front, back, front, back, front of st—5 sts.
Rows 2 and 4 Purl.
Row 3 Knit.
Row 5 K2tog, k1, k2tog—3 sts.
Row 6 P3tog.
Fasten off. Using tails, sew to center of flower. Attach flower to tag.

2. Corkscrew travel trio
Make one in each length.
Loosely cast on 10 (15, 20) sts.
Row 1 K into front, back and front of each st across—30 (45, 60) sts.
Bind off purlwise.

Following direction of spiral, tighten each corkscrew, squeezing to hold shape as you twist. Steam lightly if necessary.

Tie the 3 corkscrews together and attach to tag.

3. Traveling oak leaf
SPECIAL ABBREVIATION
Sp2p Slip1 st knitwise, p2tog, pass slipped st over just made st.
With dpns, cast on 5 sts and work I-cord (see page 123) for 1¼"/3cm.
Row 1 K1, m1, [k1, yo] twice, k1, m1, k1—9 sts.
Row 2 and all WS rows unless noted Purl.
Rows 3, 13 and 23 [K3, yo] twice, k3—11 sts.
Rows 5, 15 and 25 K3, yo, k5, yo, k3—13 sts.
Rows 7 and 17 K3, yo, k7, yo, k3—15 sts.
Rows 9 and 19 K3, yo, k9, yo, k3—17 sts.
Rows 11 and 21 K8, yo, k1, yo, k3. Place last 5 sts onto holder—14 sts rem.
Rows 12 and 22 P9. Place last 5 sts onto holder—9 sts rem.
Row 27 Ssk, k1, yo, k2tog, k3, ssk, yo, k1, k2tog—11 sts.
Row 29 Ssk, yo, k2tog, k3, ssk, yo, k2tog—9 sts.
Row 31 Ssk, yo, k2tog, k1, ssk, yo, k2tog—7 sts.
Row 33 Ssk, yo, sl 2tog kwise, k1, p2sso, yo, k2tog—5 sts.
Row 35 K1, sl 2tog kwise, k1, p2sso, k1—3 sts.
Row 36 Sp2p—1 st.
Fasten off.

LEFT-SIDE LEAF TIPS
With RS facing, place sts from upper left holder onto needle. Join yarn.
Row 1 Knit.
Rows 2 and 4 Purl.
Row 3 Ssk, k1, k2tog—3 sts.
Row 5 Sk2p—1 st.
Fasten off.
Rep for sts on lower left holder.

RIGHT-SIDE LEAF TIPS
With WS facing, place sts from upper right holder onto needle. Join yarn.
Rows 1 and 3 Purl.
Row 2 Ssk, k1, k2tog—3 sts.
Row 4 Sk2p—1 st.
Fasten off.
Rep for sts on lower right holder.
Attach leaf to tag with glue or let hang freely. ✳

Wish Upon a Scarf

MATERIALS

1 1.75oz/50g hank (each approx **78yds/71m**) of *Artyarns Beaded Silk & Sequins,* 100% silk, each in **#267 dk blue,** • **#252 lt blue,** and **#247 silver**

• Size 6 (4mm) needles, OR SIZE TO OBTAIN GAUGE
• Tapestry needle
• Purchased scarf
• Sewing needle and matching thread
• Washable fabric adhesive (optional)

NOTE Each skein makes 3 small stars and 3 large stars.

When you wish upon a scarf? You are a star maker (literally!) when you knit these stars and attach them to a purchased scarf.

EASY

Finished measurements

Purchased scarf measures 18" x 72"/45.5 x 183cm

Gauge

22 sts and 32 rows = 4"/10cm in St st on larger needles
TAKE TIME TO CHECK GAUGE

Stars

(make 18: 3 small and 3 large in each color)

RIGHT BOTTOM POINT
Cast on 2 sts.
Row 1 (RS) Knit.
Row 2 and all WS rows Purl.
Row 3 K1, m1, k to end.
Rep Rows 2 and 3 until there are 8 (10) sts on the needle, end with WS row.
Cut yarn, leaving sts on needle.

LEFT BOTTOM POINT
Cast on 2 sts to beg of needle with sts.
Row 1 (RS) Knit.
Row 2 and all WS rows Purl.
Row 3 K to last st, m1, k1.

Rep Rows 2 and 3 until there are 8 (10) sts on the needle, end with WS row.
Joining row (RS) K16 (20).
P1 row.

SIDE POINTS
Inc row (RS) K1, m1, k to last st, m1, k1—18 (22) sts.
Next row Purl.
Rep last 2 rows until there are 26 (32) sts on the needle, end with WS row.
Bind off 8 (10) sts at beg of next 2 rows—10 (12) sts.

TOP POINT
Row 1 (RS) Knit.
Row 2 and all WS rows Purl.
Rows 3, 5, 7 (and 9) K1, ssk, k to last 3 sts, k2tog, k1—4 sts after Row 7 (9).
Row 9 (11) K1, k2tog, k1—3 sts.
Row 11 (13) Sk2p—1 st.
Fasten off.

Finishing

Weave in all ends and press lightly. Place on scarf background as desired and sew (or glue) in place. ❊

● make it special
You can sew two
stars together and
stuff them with fiberfill
to create a unique
Christmas ornament
or gift embellishment.
A box full of them
can also make a
great present.

Guide to Giving

AFGHANS FOR AFGHANS

c/o AFSC Collection Center
65 Ninth Street
San Francisco, CA 94103
www.afghansforafghans.org

• Through partnerships with relief agencies Afghans for Afghans sends hand-knit and crocheted blankets, sweaters, vests, hats, mittens and socks to Afghan people suffering from oppression, war, hunger, poverty and sickness.

Items accepted: Hats, mittens, socks, blankets, sweaters and vests. Size requirements vary by specific campaigns; check the website to see what is currently most needed.

Special requirements: Items should be knit from wool or other animal fibers for warmth and durability (do not use airy or loopy stitches). Acrylic items or those made up of primarily synthetic fibers will not be accepted. Do not incorporate religious or national symbols or representational images such as faces and animals in your design—Islam prohibits depicting such likenesses.

BINKY PATROL

c/o Carolyn Berndt
19065 Ridgeview Road
Villa Park, CA 92861
(503) 214-8346
www.binkypatrol.org

• Through local chapters and Bink-a-thons, Binky Patrol provides homemade blankets to children born HIV positive, drug-addicted, infected with AIDS or other chronic and terminal illnesses, as well as to those who are abused, in foster care or experiencing trauma of any kind.

Items accepted: Blankets in all sizes from as small as two feet square up to twin-bed size.

Special requirements: All patterns are acceptable, as long as they are soft, washable and can make it through the dryer.

CARE WEAR

Bonnie Hagerman
c/o Hood College
401 Rosemont Avenue
Frederick, MD 21701
(301) 696-3550
www.carewear.org

• What began as a personal mission to provide hospitals with apparel for premature and low-birthweight babies has been expanded to a nationwide network of volunteers supplying hospitals and shelters with items for larger infants, children and even geriatric patients.

Items accepted: Hats, booties, socks, burial gowns, finger puppets, shawls, mittens, lap blankets.

Special requirements: Use yarn that may be washed in hot water with harsh detergents and disinfectants. Wool yarn may be used for blankets, but should be labeled "Wool: Wash in Cool Water" so that these are distributed to infants and families that do not suffer allergies.

CHEMO CAPS

http://chemocaps.com
e-mail: ronni@chemocaps.com

• Also known as the Heather Spoll No Hair Day Hat program, Chemo Caps was established in memory of a knitter lost to cancer at the age of 25 and makes and distributes hats for cancer patients in hospital oncology units and hospices.

Items accepted: Hats and caps.

Special requirements: Use soft, washable yarns.

CHRISTMAS AT SEA

The Seamen's Church Institute
241 Water Street
New York, NY 10038
(212) 349-9090
www.seamenschurch.org/484.asp

• A program of the Seamen's Church Institute, Christmas at Sea distributes gift packages containing handmade scarves, caps, vests, helmets or socks, as well as other items useful to deep-sea and river mariners, providing warmth and comfort to those far from home and family.

Items accepted: Caps, helmets, slippers and scarves.

Special requirements: Use the patterns supplied on the website and yarns that can be laundered. Avoid rose, pink, lavender and other pastel shades.

CUBS FOR KIDS

1 North Lexington Avenue
White Plains, NY 10601
(914) 421-4916
www.cubsforkids.com

• Cubs for Kids outfits stuffed teddy bears with hand-knit hats, sweaters and scarves, and distributes them to children in homeless shelters across the country.

Items accepted: Cubs for Kids supplies a bear and patterns for a sweater, scarf and hat in which to dress him.

Special requirements: Bears must be dressed in clothing made according to the patterns supplied.

HATS FOR THE HOMELESS

905 Main Street
Hackensack NJ 07601
e-mail: *infor@hats4thehomeless.org*
www.hats4thehomeless.org

• Created in the memory of young man who made a holiday tradition of handing out warm coverings to the homeless of New York City each winter, Hats for the Homeless, distributes hand-stitched hats, scarves and gloves to the homeless who flow through the doors of St. Francis Xavier's Soup Kitchen the weekend before Christmas.

Items accepted: Adult-sized hats, scarves, gloves and mittens.

Special requirements: Dark colors and men's sizes are preferred.

Organizations, charities and foundations that need your knitting skills

HEAD HUGGERS
1006 Auckland Way
Chester, MD 21619
(410) 643-5767
www.headhuggers.org

• Head Huggers is a network of crafters who knit, crochet and sew caps for those who've lost their hair to chemotherapy. The caps are distributed to hospitals, oncologists' offices and chemotherapy sites. Volunteers are encouraged to establish new satellite groups to make and collect chemo caps for distribution in their area, wherever it may be.

Items accepted: Handmade chemo caps; hats for kids are particularly in demand.

Special requirements: Any hat pattern is accepted. Soft, washable yarns are preferred. Include fiber content and laundering instructions with your donation.

HEARTMADE BLESSINGS
13 Hawthorne Drive
Durham NC 27712
www.heartmadeblessings.org

• Heartmade Blessings is a worldwide group of volunteers dedicated to providing handcrafted items to those suffering a loss, tragedy or illness, as a simple reminder that people care.

Items accepted: Afghans, baby blankets and 6-, 7-, or 12-inch knitted squares.

Special requirements: Squares and blankets should be made from 4-ply acrylic worsted-weight yarn. Do not use solid black. These items are sent out to those in need of comfort due to a tragedy or illness.

HELPING HANDS FOUNDATION, INC.
1100-H Brandywine Blvd.
Zanesville, OH 43701-7303
(740) 452-4541
www.needleartsmentoring.org

• Through its Needle Arts Mentoring Program, Helping Hands Foundation, Inc. pairs knitters with youngsters eager to learn needle arts, promoting and encouraging relationships between adults and youth and fostering curiosity, creativity and a feeling of achievement through the teaching of needle arts.

Items accepted: Mentors teach knitting skills to young boys and girls.

Special requirements: Mentors attend one two-hour training session and commit to meeting with their youngsters once a week for a one-hour session for six weeks.

HILTON HEAD HEROES
27 Rusty Rail Lane
Hilton Head Island, SC 29926-2560
www.hhheroes.com

• Hilton Head Heroes brings children between the ages of 4 and 18 suffering from life-threatening illnesses and their families to Hilton Head Island, South Carolina, for a resort vacation. The families are housed in the Hilton Head Island HERO house located in Sea Pines Resort.

Items accepted: Lap blankets for each Hero child. The blankets help keep the child warm while in the hospital, riding in a wheelchair, and during chemo treatments.

Special requirements: Blankets should measure 36" x 36".

I CROSS CANADA
P. O. Box 3
Saanichton BC V8M 2C3 CA
(250) 652-4137
www.icross.ca/project.htm
http://icross-canada.com

• I Cross ships medical supplies to people in developing countries. The little knit dolls placed in the boxes as packing to protect breakable items have become one of the most desired items in the box, especially for the children.

Items needed: Knitted comfort dolls.

Special requirements: Dolls are designed to protect breakable items in the shipments and must be made following a simple pattern provided on the website.

KNIT FOR THE CURE LOS ANGELES COUNTY AFFILIATE
c/o Knit for the Cure
Susan G. Komen for the Cure
1000 East Walnut Street
Suite 123
Pasadena, CA 91106-2426.

• Since 2005, Knit for the Cure has raised $20,000 for breast cancer research and treatment. Volunteers donate pink knitted items, which are sold at Susan G. Komen events or given as gifts to breast cancer patients. Funds go to the Los Angeles County Affiliate of the Susan G. Komen Foundation.

Items accepted: Scarves, bags, ponchos, hats, blankets and more.

Special requirements: The item must be pink (any shade).

THE MOTHER BEAR PROJECT
P.O. Box 62188
Minneapolis, MN 55426
www.motherbearproject.org

• With the simple gift of a hand-knit bear with a tag signed by the knitter, the Mother Bear Project gives poverty-stricken children, primarily those affected by HIV/AIDS in emerging nations, the message that they are loved by someone halfway around the world.

Items accepted: Hand-knit and crocheted bears made from a World War II-era pattern that was chosen because the bears are lightweight and easy to send.

Special requirements: Bears must be knit or crocheted by hand using the pattern supplied by the Mother Bear Project. The colors and details are the choice of the knitter. Avoid embellishing with buttons or other items that could pose a choking hazard.

NEWBORNS IN NEED

3323 Transou Road
Pfafftown, NC 27040
(877) 231-5097
www.newbornsinneed.org

• Chapters across the U.S. provide baby blankets, hats and booties to families living at or below the poverty level. Their bereavement program provides burial layettes and keepsake items.
Items accepted: Needs vary by chapter, but blankets, booties, caps and burial layettes are the most commonly created items.
Special requirements: None. Patterns are available on the Newborns in Need website, but feel free to use your own designs.

ONE HEART ONE MIND PATHWAYS TO SPIRIT

4307 Goldeneye Drive
Fort Collins, CO 80526
(970) 282-3819
www.pathwaystospirit.org

• A project of Pathways to the Spirit, a volunteer organization dedicated to the provision of material assistance to and cultural preservation of Native Americans on the reservations of South Dakota and along the Front Range of Colorado, the One Heart One Mind project reaches out to teenage mothers, providing hand-

knit items to babies born at the Lakota Tiwahe Center in Rosebud, South Dakota, an early intervention center working with parents and their newborn to 5-year-olds.
Items needed: Hats, booties, socks, mittens and knitted teddy bears.
Special requirements: None.

OPERATION LAP WRAP

USA Cares, Inc.
c/o: Operation Lap Wrap
562B N. Dixie, Suite #3
Radcliff, KY 40160
(800) 773-0387
www.usacares.org/lapWrap.htm

• Operation Lap Wrap supports injured veterans by supplying warn blankets to military personnel who've lost limbs and are confined to wheelchairs.
Items accepted: Lap wraps.
Special requirements: Finished pieces should measure no larger than 45" x 45".

OPERATION TOASTY TOES

5232 N. Ridge Rd.
Madison, OH 44057
(440) 428-6354
www.operationtoastytoes.org

• With shipments of slippers, hats, helmets and more, Operation Toasty Toes warms both the body and spirits of armed forces members stationed overseas.
Items accepted: Socks, slippers, dickeys; headbands; helmets, watchcaps and fingerless mitts knit with patterns from Toasty Toes.
Special requirements: To comply with shipping requirements and the needs of the military, items must be knit from patterns supplied by Operation Toasty Toes.

PROJECT LINUS

Project Linus National
Headquarters
P. O. Box 5621
Bloomington IL 61702-5621
(309) 664-7814
www.projectlinus.org

• Comprising hundreds of local chapters and thousands of volunteers across the United States, Project Linus provides love, a sense of security, warmth and comfort to children who are seriously ill, traumatized, or otherwise in need through the gifts of new, handmade blankets.
Items accepted: Blankets, usually 40" x 60"; local chapters may have certain preferences depending on the facilities to which they donate.
Special requirements: Blankets must be free of smoky smells or any chemicals that could cause problems for a child. Do not embellish with buttons or other items that could pose a choking hazard.

RED SCARF PROJECT

Orphan Foundation of America
The Red Scarf Project
21351 Gentry Drive
Sterling, VA 20166
(571) 203-0270
orphan.org/index.php?id=40

• A program of the Orphan Foundation of America (OFA), the Red Scarf Project sends warmth and encouragement to foster youth by putting hand-knit red scarves into Valentine care packages that are sent to OFA students enrolled in college or trade school.
Items accepted: Unisex, collegiate-style scarves in solids, stripes or patterns.

Special requirements: Scarves should be knit from soft, red (this can include burgundy, russet and other shades) DK, double fingering-weight, worsted-weight, or light-bulky yarns and measure approximately 60" long and 5" to 8" wide. Donations are limited to no more than five scarves from any one person or organization and, due to storage constraints, can only be sent during a specified time period. See the website for details.

SNUGGLES PROJECT

Hugs for Homeless Animals
P. O. Box 320245
Franklin, WI 53132-6031
(888) 483-8180
www.snugglesproject.org

• Working with Hugs for Homeless Animals, the Snuggles Project provides hand-knitted, sewn and crocheted blankets for animals in shelters across the U.S.
Items accepted: Pet blankets and cage pads for animal shelters. Volunteers can participate through local chapters or donate items on their own.
Special requirements: Needs vary by chapter and shelter, but in general items should be made from machine-washable yarn and measure 14" x 14" for cats and small animals, 24" x 24" for cats and small-to-medium dogs, 36" x 36" for medium-to-large dogs. Thicker blankets are preferred. Patterns are available on the organization's website, but volunteers are free to create their own designs.

Become a part of nationwide or local knitting charities and enrich the lives of others with your time and your skill.

SOCKS FOR SOLDIERS INC.
S 2892 State Route 96 East
Shelby, OH 44875
(419) 342-2486
www.socksforsoldiersinc.com
groups.yahoo.com/group/
socksforsoldiers

• Socks for soldiers sends hand-knitted superwash wool socks in special care packages to soldiers serving in the Middle East and Afghanistan and operates from a Yahoo! group rather than a website.
Items accepted: Black socks in simple patterns.
Special requirements: Socks must be black, knit in a wool or wool-cotton blend and high enough to go over the top of a boot by several inches.

STITCHES FROM THE HEART
3316 Pico Boulevard
Santa Monica, CA 90405
(877) 985-9212
www.stitchesfromtheheart.org

• More than 1,400 volunteers strong and growing daily, Stitches from the Heart sends handmade clothing, blankets, and love to premature babies all across the nation.
Items accepted: Booties, blankets and layette items.
Special requirements: Use soft, washable yarns; do not use 100% wool. Measurements and size requirements can be found on the website.

WARM UP AMERICA!
Craft Yarn Council of America
469 Hospital Dr., 2nd Floor Suite E
Gastonia, NC 28054
(704) 824-7838
www.warmupamerica.org

• Warm Up America! volunteers create handmade blankets that are distributed to those in need. These items provide warmth and comfort to people who have lost their homes, fled abusive relations, or are being cared for in hospices, shelters, hospitals and nursing homes.
Items accepted: 7" × 9" knitted blocks or completed blankets.
Special requirements: None

WARM WOOLIES
5572 E. Mansfield Avenue
Denver, CO 80237
www.warmwoolies.org

• Volunteers for Warm Woolies knit for children living in orphanages in Russia, Kazakhstan, China and Mongolia, and on reservations throughout the northern United States.
Items accepted: Items most needed, in order, are socks, sweaters, vests and baby blankets.
Special requirements: Items should be at least 75% animal fiber, with 100% animal fiber strongly preferred; baby blankets may be made with acrylic yarns.

WARMING FAMILIES
One Heart International
P. O. Box 400
Orem, UT 84059
www.warmingfamilies.com/mission.aspx

• Warming Families, a project of the One Heart Foundation, distributes blankets, warm clothing and other items of comfort to the homeless and displaced.
Items accepted: Blankets, bears and dolls, gloves, mittens, hats and headbands. Project needs vary by local chapter.
Special requirements: None ✳

Glossary and Techniques

Skill Levels

Beginner
Ideal first project.

Easy
Stitches, minimal shaping and simple finishing.

Intermediate
For knitters with some experience. More intricate stitches, shaping and finishing.

Experienced
For knitters able to work patterns with complicated shaping and finishing.

Abbreviations

approx	approximately
beg	begin(ning)
CC	contrasting color
ch	chain
cm	centimeter(s)
cn	cable needle
cont	continu(e)(ing)
dec	decreas(e)(ing)
dpn	double-pointed needle(s)
foll	follow(s)(ing)
g	gram(s)
inc	increas(e)(ing)
k	knit
LH	left-hand
lp(s)	loop(s)
m	meter(s)
mm	millimeter(s)
MC	main color
M1	make one
M1 p-st	make 1 purl stitch
oz	ounce(s)
p	purl
pat(s)	pattern(s)
pm	place marker
psso	pass slip stitch(es) over
rem	remain(s)(ing)
rep	repeat
RH	right-hand
RS	right side(s)
rnd(s)	round(s)
SKP	slip 1, knit 1, pass slip stitch over—one stitch has been decreased
SK2P	slip 1, knit 2 together, pass slip stitch over the knit 2 together—two stitches have been decreased
S2KP	slip 2 stitches together, knit 1, pass 2 slip stitches over knit 1
sl	slip
sl st	slip stitch
ssk	slip, slip, knit
sssk	slip, slip, slip, knit
st(s)	stitch(es)
St st	stockinette stitch
tbl	through back loop(s)
tog	together
WS	wrong side(s)
W&T	wrap & turn
wyib	with yarn in back
wyif	with yarn in front
yd	yard(s)
yo	yarn over needle
*	repeat directions following * as many times as indicated
[ ]	repeat directions inside brackets as many times as indicated

Duplicate Stitch

Duplicate stitch covers a knit stitch. Bring the needle up below the stitch to be worked. Insert the needle under both loops one row above and pull it through. Insert it back into the stitch below and through the center of the next stitch in one motion, as shown.

Kiss Me Wrap-Around
page 103

122

Glossary

bind off Used to finish an edge or segment. Lift the first stitch over the second, the second over the third, etc. (U.K.: cast off)

bind off in ribbing Work in ribbing as you bind off. (Knit the knit stitches, purl the purl stitches.) (U.K.: cast off in ribbing)

3-needle bind-off With the right side of the two pieces facing and the needles parallel, insert a third needle into the first stitch on each needle and knit them together. Knit the next two stitches the same way. Slip the first stitch on the third needle over the second stitch and off the needle. Repeat for three-needle bind-off.

cast on Placing a foundation row of stitches upon the needle in order to begin knitting.

decrease Reduce the stitches in a row (that is, knit 2 together).

increase Add stitches in a row (that is, knit in front and back of stitch).

knitwise Insert the needle into the stitch as if you were going to knit it.

make one With the needle tip, lift the strand between the last stitch knit and the next stitch on the left-hand needle and knit into back of it. One knit stitch has been added.

make one p-st With the needle tip, lift the strand between the last stitch worked and the next stitch on the left-hand needle and purl it. One purl stitch has been added.

no stitch On some charts, "no stitch" is indicated with shaded spaces where stitches have been decreased or not yet made. In such cases, work the stitches of the chart, skipping over the "no stitch" spaces.

pick up and knit (purl) Knit (or purl) into the loops along an edge.

place markers Place or attach a loop of contrast yarn or purchased stitch marker as indicated.

purlwise Insert the needle into the stitch as if you were going to purl it.

selvage stitch Edge stitch that helps make seaming easier.

slip, slip, knit Slip next two stitches knitwise, one at a time, to right-hand needle. Insert tip of left-hand needle into fronts of these stitches, from left to right. Knit them together. One stitch has been decreased.

slip, slip, slip, knit Slip next three stitches knitwise, one at a time, to right-hand needle. Insert tip of left-hand needle into fronts of these stitches, from left to right. Knit them together. Two stitches have been decreased.

slip stitch An unworked stitch made by passing a stitch from the left-hand to the right-hand needle as if to purl.

work even Continue in pattern without increasing or decreasing. (U.K.: work straight)

yarn over Making a new stitch by wrapping the yarn over the right-hand needle. (U.K.: yfwd, yon, yrn)

Three-Needle Bind-Off

This bind-off is used to join two edges that have the same number of stitches, such as shoulder edges which have been placed on holders.

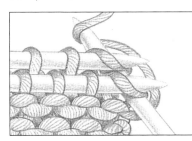

1 With the right side of the two pieces facing each other, and the needles parallel, insert a third needle knitwise into the first stitch of each needle. Wrap the yarn around the needle as if to knit.

2 Knit these two stitches together and slip them off the needles. *Knit the next two stitches together in the same way as shown.

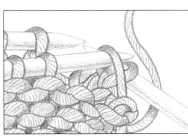

3 Slip the first stitch on the third needle over the second stitch and off the needle. Repeat from the * in step 2 across the row until all the stitches are bound off.

I-cord

Cast on about three to five stitches. *Knit one row. Without turning the work, slip the stitches back to the beginning of the row. Pull the yarn tightly from the end of the row. Repeat form the * as desired. Bind off.

**Reversible Hoodie
page 20**

Working a Yarn Over

There are different ways to make a yarn over. Which method to use depends on where you are in the stitch pattern. If you do not make the yarn over in the right way, you may lose it on the following row, or make a yarn over that is too big. Here are the different variations:

I Between two knit stitches: Bring the yarn from the back of the work to the front between the two needles. Knit the next stitch, bringing the yarn to the back over the right-hand needle, as shown.

2 Between a knit and a purl stitch: Bring the yarn from the back to the front between the two needles. Then bring it to the back over the right-hand needle and back to the front again, as shown. Purl the next stitch.

3 Between a purl and a knit stitch: Leave the yarn at the front of the work. Knit the next stitch, bringing the yarn to the back over the right-hand needle, as shown.

4 Between two purl stitches: Leave the yarn at the front of the work. Bring the yarn to the back over the right-hand needle and to the front again, as shown. Purl the next stitch.

5 Multiple yarn overs (two or more): Wrap the yarn around the needle, as when working a single yarn over, then continue wrapping the yarn around the needle as many times as indicated. Work the next stitch of the left-hand needle. On the following row, work stitches into the extra yarn overs as described in the pattern. The illustration above right depicts a finished yarn over on the purl side.

Kitchener Stitch

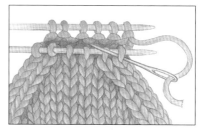

I Insert tapestry needle purlwise (as shown) through first stitch on front needle. Pull yarn through, leaving that stitch on knitting needle.

2 Insert tapestry needle knitwise (as shown) through first stitch on back needle. Pull yarn through, leaving stitch on knitting needle.

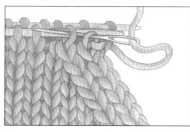

3 Insert tapestry needle knitwise through first stitch on front needle, slip stitch off needle and insert tapestry needle purlwise (as shown) through next stitch on front needle. Pull yarn through, leaving this stitch on needle.

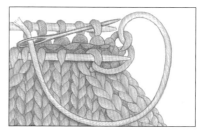

4 Insert tapestry needle purlwise through first stitch on back needle. Slip stitch off needle and insert tapestry needle knitwise (as shown) through next stitch on back needle. Pull yarn through, leaving this stitch on needle. Repeat steps 3 and 4 until all stitches on both front and back needles have been grafted. Fasten off and weave in end.

How to Make a Pompom

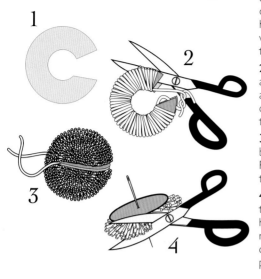

1 With two circular pieces of cardboard the width of the desired pompom, cut a center hole. Then cut a pie-shaped wedge out of the circle. (Use the picture as a guide.)

2 Hold the two circles together and wrap the yarn tightly around the cardboard. Then carefully cut around the cardboard.

3 Tie a piece of yarn tightly between the two circles. Remove the cardboard and trim the pompom.

4 Sandwich pompom between two round pieces of cardboard held together with a long needle. Cut around the circumference for a perfect pompom.

Beading

When threading beads onto yarn, the needle must be large enough to accommodate the yarn, but small enough to go through the beads. You can use an auxilliary thread, as shown here. Loop the thread through a folded piece of yarn and pull both ends through.

To add beads in stockinette stitch on right-side rows, beads are placed without the purl stitches on either side. The bead will lie directly in front of the stitch. Work the stitch firmly so that the bead won't fall to the back of the work.

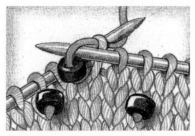

From the right side: Work to the stitch to be beaded, then slip the bead up in back of the work. Insert needle as if to knit; wrap yarn around it. Push bead to front through the stitch on the left needle; complete the stitch.

Embroidery Stitches

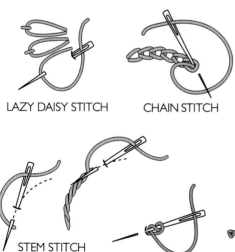

LAZY DAISY STITCH   CHAIN STITCH

STEM STITCH

FRENCH KNOT

STRAIGHT STITCH

Meow Kitty Cap
page 30

Ruched Mitts
page 66

Single Crochet

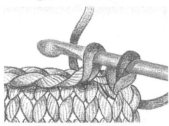

1 Draw through a loop as for a slip stitch, bring the yarn over the hook, and pull it through the first loop. *Insert the hook into the next stitch and draw through a second loop.

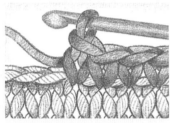

2 Yarn over and pull through both loops on the hook. Repeat from the * to the end.

All Heart Shawl
page 40

Yarn and Materials Sources

Artyarns
39 Westmoreland Avenue
White Plains, NY 10606
www.artyarns.com

Berroco, Inc.
P. O. Box 367
14 Elmdale Road
Uxbridge, MA 01569
www.berroco.com

Brown Sheep Company
100662 County Road 16
Mitchell, NE 69357
www.brownsheep.com

Blue Sky Alpacas
P. O. Box 88
Cedar, MN 55011
www.blueskyalpacas.com

Cascade Yarns
1224 Andover Park East
Tukwila, WA 98188
www.cascadeyarns.com

Classic Elite Yarns
122 Western Avenue
Lowell, MA 01851
www.classiceliteyarns.com

Coats & Clark
3430 Toringdon Way, Suite 301
Charlotte NC 28277
www.coatsandclark.com

Crystal Palace
160 23rd Street
Richmond, CA 94804
www.crystalpalaceyarns.com

Deanna's Vintage Styles
2134 Van Antwerp
Grosse Pointe, MI 48326
www.vintagestyles.com

Fairmount Fibers, Ltd.
P. O. Box 2082
Philadelphia, PA 19103
www.fairmountfibers.com

Filatura Di Crosa
Distributed by
Tahki•Stacy Charles, Inc.

GGH
Distributed by Muench Yarns

Homestead Heirlooms
(262)352-8738
www.homesteadheirlooms.com

Interlacements
18 Dillon Creek Road
Raton, NM 87740
interlacementsyarns.com

Jade Sapphire Exotic Fibres
(866)857-3897
www.jadesapphire.com

JHB International, Inc.
1955 South Quince Street
Denver, CO 80231
www.buttons.com

Knitpicks
1(800) 574-1323
www.knitpicks.com

Lane Borgosesia
Distributed by
Trendsetter Yarns

Lion Brand Yarn
34 West 15th Street
New York, NY 10011
www.lionbrand.com

Lorna's Laces
4229 North Honore Street
Chicago, IL 60613
www.lornaslaces.net

Manos del Uruguay
Distributed by
Fairmount Fibers, Ltd.
www.manos.com.uy

Mission Falls
5333 Casgrain #1204
Montreal, Quebec
H2T 1X3 Canada
www.missionfalls.com

Muench Yarns, Inc.
1323 Scott Street
Petaluma, CA 94954-1135
www.muencharns.com

The Old Mill Knitting Co.
P. O. Box 81176
Ancaster, Ontario
L9G 4X2 Canada
www.oldmillknitting.com

Rowan
Distributed by
Westminster Fibers, Inc.
www.knitrowan.com
UK: Green Lane Mill
Holmfirth
HD9 2DX England
www.knitrowan.com

RYC
Distributed by
Westminster Fibers, Inc.

Sunbelt Fastener Company
www.sunbeltfastener.com

Swarovski Elements (Crystallized)
www.crystallized.com

Tahki•Stacy Charles, Inc.
70-30 80th Street, Building 36
Ridgewood, NY 11385
www.tahkistacycharles.com

Tahki Yarns
Distributed by
Tahki•Stacy Charles, Inc.

Trendsetter Yarns
16745 Saticoy Street
Suite #101
Van Nuys, CA 91406
www.trendsetteryarns.com
Canada: Distributed by
The Old Mill Knitting Company

Unicorn Books & Crafts
1318 Ross Street
Petaluma, CA 94954
www.unicornbooks.com

Westminster Fibers
165 Ledge Street
Nashua, NH 03060
www.westminsterfibers.com

Windy Valley Muskox
9523 N. Wolverine Road
Palmer, AK 99645
www.windyvalleymuskox.net

acknowledgments

Thank you to the
staff at Sixth& Spring
for their help in putting
this gift book together.
Their time and talent were
a gift to me. Trisha Malcolm,
Joe Vior, Diane Lamphron, Tanis Gray, Faith Hale,
Carla Scott, Lori Steinberg, Lisa Buccellato, Sarah
DeVita, Michelle Bredeson and my favorite 24/7
full-support editor Wendy Williams.

Thank you to Rose Callahan and Jack Deutsch
for their always beautiful photography.

Thanks to my wonderful knitters,
Deanna Van Assche, Jo Brandon, Claire Brenner,
Sue Colistra, Eileen Curry, Nancy Henderson,
Julie Hines, Holly Neiding, Maggie McManus,
Mary Taylor and Eva Wilkens, who make my life
easier. Also, thanks to Heris Stenzel and
Daryl Brower. And, finally, thanks to Howard, my
favorite traveling companion and writer.

Praise to all the generous knitters out there
who give so much of their time and creativity to
knitting for charities, and to the many yarn
companies who donate yarn and needles to
special groups that knit for charities.

Blessed are the knit-givers, for they shall
know the true joy of knitting!

Knits & Kisses Forever! Love, Nicky